Heaven Won't Wait

by

Paul Gruzalski

To Gill, my patient wife who is wondering why I am still a starving writer. And to Mary Merrett who proofread this book.

PREFACE

I'm not making any claim about knowing what happens after one dies, and I do not even have any special knowledge not even a near-death experience. The place described where people arrive after the destruction of Haversay is not an attempt to portray what some people call Purgatory. It is just a place between heaven and hell where people can observe their lives in proper perspective: a place to reflect and see the affect of their lives while on Earth, before choosing where to go next. Yes, here they can choose!

Chapter 1

MAGGIE O'HARE'S FUNERAL

We go about our lives worrying about all sorts of things: where our next meal is coming from, losing one's job, and serious sickness. Also, things not so important: what to wear the next day, keeping the boss happy, what gift to buy for a birthday, what to cook for dinner, who to invite for a party, and whether to get that second computer. All worries, big and small would become insignificant if we knew for certain that soon we would be no longer on this Earth. Thankfully, we don't know when we will be called to the next world and neither did anyone in the village of Haversay-by-the Sea even though most of them would soon be gone! If they had known they were going, one wonders if they would have spent their last few days any differently.

Haversay-by-the Sea was a small village in Cornwall with only a dozen or so shops facing the sea and a very small harbour where a few fishing boats were anchored. The harbour was the reason for the village, the fishing and the sea that brought a living and sudden death: a year would hardly go by without another fisherman or tourist dying in the sea near the harbour. Offshore business had always been historically associated with this village and its small hidden harbour that once had been the haven of several notorious pirates and smugglers. There were whispers that smuggling still went on; this time the contraband was drugs. Furthermore, it was suggested that this was the reason there was a full-service bank in the small village because, so the rumour went, of certain offshore business connected to the Mafia's drug business but nothing ever had been proven

The village had the usual shops: a butchers, a bakery, hairdressers, antique shop, one small supermarket and a post office which the government threatened to close every year. Unusually, it had one very exclusive restaurant that was so expensive that none of the locals could afford it. Of course, there was a pub appropriately filled with old anchors and ropes boasting the village's past fishing history its large beams and low roof revealing its age. Here the locals gathered to exchange gossip and to partake of in a few pints of beer. It was a quiet village where many came to retire. It had both a Catholic Church and an Anglican Church.

It was September and the villagers were well prepared for the October 'hurricane' season: sandbags and boarding for the windows were stocked and ready to use. Of course the Met Office did not officially call this time of year the hurricane season: they called the October storm two years ago, and the October storm the previous year, gales and denied that it was anything but a coincidence that these savage storms, with winds up to hundred miles an hour were hurricanes! This was despite climatologists predicting such storms would increase both in frequency and in intensity. It was the year sea levels had risen by six cm worldwide, more rapidly than any of the scientists had predicted. But these global events seemed to pass the villagers by they were concerned with more local issues.

The present concern in the village was the death of the local recluse, Maggie O'Hare. Since she had no known family, one would have thought that the attendance at her funeral would be small. Amazingly, over three quarters of the villagers turned up. The reason why so many came was the disclosure that Maggie had an estate worth over two million pounds. In addition, Maggie's solicitor had asked a dozen of the village's residents to attend the reading of her will. Nobody knew who had received letters except Mr. Snives, Haversay's only solicitor, and he, for professional reasons, could not divulge how many of the villagers the will named.

Most of those who received a letter were surprised since they had never spoken to or had any dealings with Maggie. One of the few who had spoken to her was the window cleaner John Humpkin. The other was a gardener and handyman Tom Wallace, and of course, there was Father Michael Murphy, the Catholic priest.

One lady who received a letter was very mystified that Maggie had mentioned her in the will. When she was alive, Maggie might have had legal grounds to sue Veronica Stillwater for libel. Veronica had told numerous people in the village that she had seen a man and perhaps several men enter Maggie's house late at night on a number of occasions. Her information caused some of the other villagers to refer to Maggie as a loose woman. She had such a reputation that wives made sure their husbands did not head in the direction of her cottage if they desired to go anywhere in the evening.

Veronica was suspicious of the authenticity of the letter and called Mr. Snives himself to verify that there was no mistake. His answer was even more mystifying.

"Yes, Miss Stillwater. You're mentioned in the will and it would most certainly be in your interest to be there for the reading."

Veronica puzzled over this as she dressed for the funeral. She had a special outfit for such an occasion. She wore black from head to foot including a black veil, as only a lady should when attending a funeral. She was at odds, though, with that Irish priest who insisted on what he called the new rites of the sacraments even wearing white robes for every funeral emphasising the joys of the resurrection rather than emphasising that death was painful and full of grief, which good tradition always upheld. If that wasn't bad enough the silly priest wanted people to shake hands in the middle of Mass and even smile at one another while wishing each other the peace of Christ. Didn't the man know that religion was a private thing between you and your God!

Father Murphy had to make all the arrangements for Maggie's funeral. In fact, he and Maggie planned it when she knew she was dying. He was one of the few people who had been in her cold dark cottage in the winter evenings. Mr. Snives assured him that there was plenty of money to cover any expenses. He was the executor for the estate having been given explicit guidelines by Mrs. O'Hare as to how the will should be read.

Father Murphy was having the usual difficulty getting his vestments on. His problem was that he was much shorter and, let's say, slightly rounder than the previous priest. His sacristan, Bill, was just going out to light the candles when he shot back in again: "Father Murphy, you must look at the size of our congregation today. You 'd think it was Christmas."

Father Murphy usually did have a quick look at the congregation before Mass began so that he could gauge his homily. Today he had planned a very short sermon for the few that might, he thought, be present. He went to the sacristy door and opened it slightly. Bill was right. The church was packed. And wasn't that Veronica Stillwater boldly sitting in the front pew. He decided then to change his sermon from the vague generalities he was going to present to one which was more relevant to the congregation before him.

"Why are all these people here, Father?" Bill scratched the top of his balding head while looking down at the rotund priest. Whenever Bill, who was thin as a weed, served Mass with Father Murphy they contrasted comically.

"It could be because they know the lady was rich, and they've come to find out what I know about her. One thing is certain. They're not here because they miss Maggie. Now you must light the candles Bill and then come and join me at the back of the church where we will lead in the remains of poor Mrs O'Hare. This congregation will not get the homily they want, they will receive the homily they deserve."

As Father Murphy walked up the main aisle, he watched those in the church discretely looking at the coffin. He could see the curiosity oozing from their eyes. Truly all the main members of the community were there even the local 'Mafia'. That's how people referred to Mr. Dan Radcliff and his two well dressed friends. He had an exclusive restaurant; so expensive that none of the local could afford going there. It' there that it is alleged he conducted his discreet business deals. It was also rumoured that he had the local bank manager in his pocket.

Father Murphy wondered how many of the people present Maggie had named in the will. Peter Biggs and his wife and three boys were there. Father felt sorry for the three boys since they suffered the taunts of the other children as he had done when he was a child because he too had been overweight. It wasn't their fault. Their surname was somewhat unfortunate since the other children, when they saw them coming, shouted, "Here comes the Biggs the three little pigs."

On the opposite side of the church were Ruth and Ronald Wright with their lovely daughters Betty and Anne. They were all tall and graceful. But they would never stay on the same side of the church as the Biggs. It was Peter Biggs who had foreclosed on their mortgage after Ronald was made redundant, forcing them to find other accommodation. It was the first and only such case in Haversay even through the notorious late 80's and the early 90's when foreclosures occurred at a rate of thousand a month.

I wonder who isn't here, thought Father Murphy.

John Humpkin read the Psalm, "The Lord is My Shepherd". He was one of the few people who would speak to Maggie. She told Father Murphy how he would joke with her as if she was one of his mates. He was a gentle accepting soul. John was surprised that Father asked him to read at Maggie's funeral since he had never read in church before. Father's response was simple: "She liked you, John. She would've wanted you to do it."

The gospel was introduced by the congregation saying, "Alleluia, alleluia! Give thanks to the risen Lord. Give praise to his name. God has proclaimed a just reward - life for us all, Alleluia."

Father placed the scriptures on the podium and began to read.

The Gospel reading was from John 14: 1- 6 *"Jesus said to his disciples,*

>   *'Do not let your hearts be troubled. Trust in God and trust in me. There are many rooms in my Father's house; if there were not, I should have told you…*
>
>   *Jesus said: 'I am the Way the Truth and the Life. No one come to the Father except through me.'"*

"This is the Gospel of the Lord," intoned Father Murphy.

"Praise to you Lord Jesus Christ," responded the congregation.

Father Murphy looked around the church before he spoke. He asked God's grace for he knew some of the people there had never entered a Catholic Church before:

"Looking around the church today I see a few people who may be a bit uneasy perhaps because you have never been in a Catholic Church before. Don't worry we promise not to lock you in! I would like to make a few relevant points about today's gospel."

Father Murphy was a gifted speaker and he knew his opening statements would lull his captive audience to relax and turn to their own thoughts, but not for long.

"We all have to face death sooner or later. Isn't that true, Mr. Radcliff." Mr. Radcliff's attention was suddenly riveted on the audacious priest. His bodyguards looked at him as if waiting for instruction that would send the priest to his eternity.

"Would you also agree, Mr. Biggs?" The congregation swung around in the direction of the nervous bank manager.

"And would you also agree, Miss Stillwater?" Now the congregation's eyes shot back to Father Murphy anxious not to hear their name next.

"Life is too fragile a thing. In fact, some people never understand what it is all about. Perhaps they become cynical and join with many others who say that it's a dog-eat-dog world and I'm the one who's going to do the eating." He looked directly at Mr. Radcliff who wasn't sure where to put his eyes.

"It may be that success is their answer to what life means." Mr. Biggs' head was well down now, but he was hanging on every word the priest said.

"Some may be just interested in looking good." This statement caused half the women and young men to put their heads down.

"Or they just may enjoy other people suffering because they are unhappy. Of course neither of the above is what Christ meant when he said, 'I am the Way, the Truth and the Life.' Christ was a person who was concerned especially with the outcasts of society. He was criticised because he associated with tax collectors and prostitutes.

"Jesus only invites us to change. He will never force us. We have a choice.

There are two roads and two choices. I believe that even after people die some would still choose the path to death. As we live our lives so we shall die." He paused and looked sadly at the congregation.

"It's not easy being a Christian but for me and for many others it's the only life worth living. To my knowledge, Maggie was a good Christian. There are some here who thought they knew her, and they thought it was proper to label her as a loose woman. And to my shame they are members of my own congregation who have used idle gossip to solidify this untrue claim." Here he stopped and looked directly at Miss Stillwater who he knew was the worst of the gossips. Miss Stillwater now lowered her head in fear that Father would call her name again. Father continued:

"Maggie was simply a woman who was deeply hurt when she was young. I cannot tell you all the details, but I can state she was terribly wronged. That is why she was a recluse: she no longer trusted her fellow humans. Maggie suffered very much with cancer, which eventually killed her. The accusations that gossips hurled against her were totally unfounded. Perhaps those of you who have hurt her with your gossip will use the rest of this Mass to ask God's forgiveness, a God who wants everyone to be with him for all eternity."

It was a half-an hour later and only seven people gathered to witness the burial: Father Murphy, Bill the sacristan, John Humpkins who washed her windows, Charlotte who owned a hairdressers, and a beautiful young lady unknown to Father Murphy.

Father Murphy went back to the presbytery to think over the day's events. The sky was dark and yet another gale was threatening. A lone black raven was perched on the house. It seemed as if it was looking down on him with evil contempt as if to say how useless he was and what he did.

"Go away you ugly bird!" He picked up a stone, but the bird was in flight before he could throw it. What a silly old man I am. That bird is one of God's creatures. It's my thoughts that are disturbing me. It angers and saddens me how a lonely broken woman could be so wrongfully accused by members of my church. What I need is a glass or two of sherry to cheer me up. He opened the door to his empty house. He did wonder sometimes if his choice of living alone was the right one. Like many priests, despite what they witness in real life, he imagined himself with an affectionate wife and family. In his own family though, he had known strife and discord. His parents constantly battled for no apparent reason. It left him vulnerable in his relationships with others. Perhaps that's why I never married, he thought.

But his faith, though not perfect, was at the core of his life. In some ways, he liked funerals. Not because he enjoyed people suffering, but because it made people aware of what life was all about: that there was more to life than what we saw' and that God and love were at the centre of its meaning. What he didn't know was that he would never have a proper funeral and his death would have much to do with the beautiful woman he had seen at the funeral.

Chapter 2

MARY PRESTON

It was the day after the funeral and a week before the reading of the will. Fr. Murphy had just finished his Sunday lunch, an Irish stew. He enjoyed cooking and quite often invited guests to dinner, but today he was content to sit and read and take a long siesta. His only other companion in the presbytery was his cat Daniel, a pure black regal beast that demanded the best of treatment that, in Fr. Murphy's own time, he received.

Fr. Murphy was always available to his parishioners and enjoyed company as well as being alone. He had plenty to do with his writing and reading. He wasn't just an academic, he would, if he could, devote his life to the poor. But this devotion had nearly cost him his life. He had nearly worked himself to death in a parish in Battersea where the needs were great and the resources too little. Working eighteen hours a day had put him into the hospital with mental and physical exhaustion. After he had been discharged, he was banished to a remote Cornwall village to recover. When his Bishop deemed him ready, he might be sent back to a parish where he could do the work he thought was so necessary. The Bishop had said he must learn to slow down and trust other people and God to do the work he couldn't do. And this Sunday he was trying to do just that.

He was just drifting off when he heard a light knocking on his door. No one he knew knocked in that fashion. Therefore, it wasn't Mrs. Harris asking about the arrangements for next week's flowers. That blessed woman takes up more of my time than it takes to buy, cut and arrange the flowers, thought Father Murphy.

He opened the door and there was the young attractive woman he had seen at the funeral. She had dark brown eyes and bold strong features reminding him of someone he knew. He used to play a guessing game with his assistant in the other parish. An actor or actress would be on television and he would guess who in the parish they looked liked. It was amazing how often they would both agree. Who do I know that looks like this girl, he asked himself?

"Hello, my name is Mary Preston. I was wondering if I could talk to you for a moment or two."

"Certainly, come in." Fr. Murphy wished that his house was a bit tidier. Books and papers lined the entrance hall. The kitchen was filled with dirty dishes and the sitting room had several books open as well as the Sunday newspaper.

"Please forgive me for the state of my house. Mondays are cleaning days so I let things pile up until then. Would you like a cup of tea? I was about to make one for myself."

"Thank you, that's very kind of you."

"Would you like to sit here?" He pulled a handful of papers off one of the sofa-chairs. He went into the kitchen and prepared the tea. Usually when he made the tea his mind would clear and he could remember things he found difficult, but today it wasn't working. Who is this woman? I know the face, but from where? I wish I had a better memory for faces and names. God you should grant every priest with this gift.

"Here's the tea," he said as he brought it in. He looked in vain for somewhere to put it down. He finally located the table under three books and a stack of last week's newsletters.

"This is really terrible. Could you hold this one moment while I clear my coffee table?" He handed her the tray and quickly put the books and papers on the floor.

"Well what can I do for you? "He sat down in a chair opposite Mary still a bit flustered and embarrassed by his untidiness. This lass must be Irish and from the West coast too. He noted her dark complexion, deep brown eyes and black thick hair. None of my Irish relatives are as dark as she.

"I wonder, could you tell me all you are able to about Maggie O'Hare? You might say I am related to her and just discovered that fact when Mr. Snives called me."

"Now I can see who it is you look like. You look like Maggie O'Hare. Are you...?"

"Yes, I'm her daughter."

"I only found out a week ago when I heard of her death. It's really a shock to discover that you are someone else's child. I dearly love my foster parents and always will think of them as my real parents. They told me that I had been adopted because they wanted me very much. I've often wondered who my real mother was. As I grew older, I understood more about the problems of unwanted pregnancies and the desire for some to have abortions for no reason other than the embarrassment or inconvenience of having a baby. At least my mother had chosen not to abort me."

Father Murphy saw that the young lady was on the verge of crying. He waited for her to continue her story.

"I learnt from Mr. Snives that she put me up for adoption as soon as I was born. She wasn't allowed to know who my foster parents were. It was only after she had hired a detective that she discovered where I was. She didn't want to upset my life. She wanted to let me know why she put me up for adoption. My parents only told me of this after the letter and call from Mr. Snives."

"You just discovered who your real mother was after she had died?"

"Yes, and I'm sad that I never had a chance to talk to her. In the letter Mr. Snives gave me he told me about Maggie, my mother. The poor lady suffered greatly. My father, who I will never know, was an itinerant carpenter. Mother and he fell in love. When she became pregnant her father insisted that she have an abortion and never see the carpenter again. Thanks to her father, my grandfather, the carpenter disappeared, but she refused to kill me. So, her father sent her away to have me and then gave her enough money to live a year and said he never wanted to see her again. She was disinherited. Her brother, my uncle Donald, never lost contact with my mother. He went to see her at least once a month and after he had died, she discovered that she was left with all the family money that was quite considerable. But that's all I know about her. I was wondering if you could tell me more.

"I'll try to tell you what I know. I knew her both as a confessor and friend. She came here to get away from people. She was hurt many times in her life. But life brought her several other blows. She lived in Surrey for a while and had a small coffee shop. She set up the business with the money her brother had left her. She was quite happy and even confident enough to start another relationship. She was seeing a man, a civil engineer, who travelled a lot. He had asked her to marry him and she, with some anxiety, said yes. Unfortunately, she discovered he had been unfaithful to her. He used his frequent travelling to hide his affair with another woman. She has been a most unluckily woman when it comes to men."

"I wish I could have brought some joy into her life." Mary's voice trailed off as her emotions took over. "I would have been her friend. I just know it. I was so sad to hear that she had no one. We could have done things together. I could have shared so much with her."

Father Murphy felt the girl's anguish and wanted to help her all he could. "I think you did make her happier. I'm sure she knew that you were happy, and it was because of her decision not to have an abortion that you were alive. But it would have been difficult for both you and your parents, especially your adopted mother, if she had made herself known to you. I have counselled several young women who were adopted and one who actually found her mother. Sadly, her mother didn't want to know. She had no place in her mother's new life."

"I suppose you're right. It would have been difficult to have two mothers especially on special occasions like Mother's Day and Christmas. What else can you tell me about my mother?"

"She was a very sensitive and gentle person. She told me about that man who hurt her so badly. She had given up on people after that and found it difficult to forgive. I told her she would be happier if she forgave him, but she said she couldn't. This was the very thing, sadly, that stopped her from living a full life."

"Is there anything else you could tell me."

"Yes, she was a very generous person who only gave anonymously. I wanted to tell those attending her funeral about her generosity, but I knew it wouldn't be right. She didn't want people to know. The local library received 2000 pounds from her. She loved literature and books. She told me she read a book about every two days."

"I love reading too but don't seem to get the time these days."

Father Murphy paused for a moment trying to think what to say next." She did have a secret hobby and that was writing. She let me see some of her short stories. I think she had a talent."

"Do you think I could see them?"

"My dear, it is only right that you should have them. I have them right here." Fr. Murphy got up to get Mary her mother's stories. He thought that he should have proof of her identity before handing over Maggie's stories, but who would want to take them anyway. True he thought they were good enough to be published, but he was no professional. He came back into the room and handed her the stories.

"You really must read them. You'll see how good they are and possibly you might get one or two of them published."

"Well thank you for the cup of tea and your time. I'll read one while I'm here and we'll compare notes. Well see you soon then." When they reached the door Mary remembered something she wanted to ask Fr. Murphy.

"Oh, by the way have you ever eaten in the *El Faro*? I met the owner at my mother's, funeral, a Mr. Dan Radcliff, he invited me to dinner. He says he doesn't see many cultured people out here. I think he really thought I would believe that line."

"Miss Preston, be careful. I fear the man is not very nice. Some believe he's the head of the local Mafia. He doesn't have bodyguards for decoration."

"Thank you for the tea and warning Father. Tomorrow we'll make a date to discuss a story."

Fr. Murphy was looking forward to their meeting. Somehow he felt they would never meet again. He was thinking about

Radcliff. I think the girl is too confident she can handle an experienced criminal like Radcliff. You know Lord that if I went over the top in warning her, she would think I was exaggerating.

"Please send your angels to watch over her," he prayed. Later he would wonder why God had not answered his prayer.

Chapter 3

THE DRUG RUNNERS

The restaurant owned by Dan Radcliff, El *Faro,* specialised in Spanish food. There was very little market for such food in Cornwall but apparently it didn't faze Radcliff. He liked Spanish food and often went on business trips to Spain or the Canary Islands. He would quite frequently sail to Spain from Haversay's little harbour when the weather was good. It was September, and one small gale had already passed through the village with winds reaching sixty miles per hour. Small vessels travelled with great care this time of year: a storm only two weeks ago had caught two fishing boats killing all those onboard.

It was just the type of weather, with temperatures up in the sixty's, that had brought on the big gales for the previous two years. According to Radcliff, it was the best time to move his cargo from the Canary Islands to England. Across the Atlantic, another indicator was present. Janet, a hurricane of immense strength had just struck the coast of Florida creating five billion dollars worth of damage and killing over three hundred people: it was the US.' worst hurricane to date. Its remnants were heading towards the western coast of the UK. Given such conditions, the Coast Guard's main concern would be for ships safety, not looking for smugglers.

Dan Radcliff knew the C.I.D. were watching him, as he knew they tapped into the phone lines to his flat above the restaurant. Knowing this, he only used mobile phones. He had three and hoped that he could get a message to his connections in the Canary Island without C.I.D. intercepting his call. He had a code that told his contacts when to move any shipment. If they sailed to Haversay, they would have to come at night and in almost complete radio silence with no lights. With the present weather, it would be nearly impossible. He was the only one in Haversay who knew where, when and how the drugs were coming to England. In various parts of the country, he had men prepared to collect the drugs on arrival. He planned to smuggle in the drugs under the noses of the C.I.D. He no longer needed the money: it was the power and the chase that excited him particularly in out guessing Inspector Maxwell.

He was talking to Peter Biggs who was his bank manager: "What's the problem, Peter? Isn't my money any good?" Peter was not an assertive man and he pretended not to know where the large sums of money came from that Radcliff deposited in his bank. He was worried because his bank was due for an inspection. His voice squeaked when he became excited.

"Mr. Radcliff, I really don't want to cause any difficulties. It's just that the sums of money, which I have been banking for you, are way in excess of what this restaurant obviously earns. The inspectors will see this and then they might ask for a further investigation. I am sure you don't want that."

"Peter, my boy. Why do you think I pay you so much? You are supposed to take care of such things. It's your job to make sure the inspectors don't ask any questions. I could get someone else for the job if you don't think you can handle it. Use your imagination. Initiate some creative accounting. Now would you like to have a meal in our restaurant? We do need the business as you well know."

Peter Biggs stood uncertain for a moment, shook his head and left the restaurant. He was a coward; though he feared the bank inspectors discovering his money laundering, he was even more frightened of crossing Radcliff. The previous bank manager walked off a cliff one stormy night, or so the story goes. Biggs thought it was more than a coincidence that he had an argument with Radcliff just before he disappeared. No, Biggs would rather face ten bank inspectors than Radcliff.

The C.I.D. had posted men one mile away from the restaurant. They had two electronic trackers monitoring Radcliff's calls.

"I think I've got something here. Listen to this," said one of the detectives. He played back the tape from the tracker. It was clear Radcliff's voice. "I think it's time I came down to do some fishing."

Inspector Maxwell listened saying nothing for a long time. He had been trying to put Dan Radcliff behind bars for three years. He well knew that Radcliff was probably aware that he was monitoring his phone calls. The statement was obviously an indication that he was moving something. But why was he making it so obvious? It was two years ago that he thought he had Radcliff. One of his trucks had picked up something from his boat when it harboured in Beer. When the police stopped and searched it all they found was a crate of leather belts with the proper papers. Radcliff had not only made a fool of Maxwell, but he managed to bring into the country three kilos of heroin on another boat from the Canary Islands.

"He's playing a game with us. He's so confident that he is informing us that he intends to bring in the drugs soon. How or where is the problem? It could be by plane or boat and he knows that unless I am sure I won't stop him. Let's hope we get lucky. See if he tries to give us a hint of how it is coming in. Perhaps he will become too cocky, or it could be that by now he is desperate to get another shipment to England. After all it's been over six months since he's tried anything."

"That's as far as we know, Inspector," replied a too talkative sergeant. The cold grey eyes of the Inspector faced the apprehensive sergeant: "I do know what I'm talking about sergeant. I hope you can accept that."

"Yes, sir. I'm sure you're right."

Radcliff smiled to himself when he put down the phone. I hope that fool Maxwell got the message. It will give the little man something to ponder. Radcliff himself was a tall distinguished looking man unlike the short wiry Maxwell. He had used his good looks as a young man to attract well-heeled middle-aged woman he met in Chelsea. He never pretended to have money but offered himself as a personal escort to the highest bidder.

He grew up in Battersea with his five brothers and two sisters. His father was a good mechanic who was manager of a garage there. Two of his older brothers joined their father learning the trade. Dan preferred to keep his hands clean. He always had money, which bothered his father, but Dan claimed to have a part time job in Chelsea with a painter who would always meet him there. Dan would wear his work clothes and then change into his smart clothes after he arrived.

Dan liked the life his rich lady friends led. He wanted the same and decided to do anything he could to achieve it. He got into the drug business through one of his lady friends who was a light user. He offered to purchase the drugs for her for a small commission. He later got other customers and started making good money. He could afford to bargain with the dealers because he wasn't a user.

He killed his first man when he was nineteen. A pusher, who also was a user, accused him of taking his customers away. He had him cornered in an alley. Dan told him he was just buying drugs for friends.

"I've just got a lot of friends," he said jokingly.

The pusher didn't think it was funny, so he attacked Dan with a knife. Dan was a good street fighter and he easily got the better of the man and in the struggle stabbed him in the stomach. The man laid on the ground bleeding to death begging for help. Dan's only thought was for himself. If he got help for this unfortunate man, the police might discover that he sold drugs. He coldly calculated that if he left him there in the alley there might be a chance that someone would find him. No, he must die and quickly. The man was still conscious when Dan slit his throat. He had no pity for the man he killed. Rather he enjoyed the thoughts that he had the guts to kill a man. With that act he had crossed the line from a mixed-up crook to a hardened criminal. He soon lost contact with his family who he thought were losers. This man was dining with Mary Preston that night.

As Dan walked out of his flat, he met his two bodyguards, Pedro and Miguel. Neither spoke good English and this was to Dan's liking since he wanted them to know as little as possible about what was going on. In fact, most of the staff spoke only

Spanish except a few of the waitresses who were local girls, good looking but not too bright. Dan liked to be in control of his people.

" Miguel, Pedro, yo no puedo comer comigo esta noche. Porque comere con una señorita hermosa."

He patted them affectionately on the back winking as he told them he was eating with a beautiful young lady that evening. They went off to their own meals.

Mary was quite impressed with *El Faro*. Her eyes first focused on the coloured fountain on the lower floor of the restaurant. It flowed into a crystal blue pool in which large colourful fish swam. Surrounding the fountain was a floor that was composed of perfectly fitting paving stones of all shapes. The tables of the restaurant, which bordered the mini plaza, were interspersed among large flowering cacti giving the effect that they were outdoors. The tables furthest from the fountain had a view of the now ever rising sea. A dimly lit second tier or balcony had fewer tables.

A beautiful señorita dressed in a long tight black dress came to greet her. Her dark hair and her flashing black eyes gave Mary no doubt that she was genuine Spanish.

"*Buenas noches, señorita.*" Mary started to speak in Spanish but stopped. I'm Mary Preston. Radcliff is expecting me. Mary's poise and looks easily matched that of the Spanish girl. Mary always was at ease with other people no matter how important or ordinary they were. Her parents had treated all people equally. That is to say, they treated all people with dignity.

As far as she was concerned a good-looking man had asked her out to a Spanish restaurant where she was intending to eat anyway. Still she was happy to be in such an exotic looking place.

"Señor Radcliff say that if you like you can chose where you like to seat. I will let him know that you are here."

The girl obviously found English very difficult. "Thank you very much."

There was no need for the girl to tell Radcliff that Mary was there. He was watching her through a one-way window, which looked like a mirror on the restaurant side. He wanted to watch Mary to see if he could learn something about her. Firstly, she was a young lady who wanted to and could make her own decisions. It took her no time to find the table she liked best. It was the one he would have chosen, the one that had a view of the moonlit sea as well as the fountain and mini plaza. Yes, and she moved with such poise. He liked what he saw.

A waitress had already brought over the menu before Dan had arrived.

"Buenas noches señorita."

"Buenas noches señor," she replied easily.

"Hablas español bien. Tu accento es perfecto" Mary did not reply to Dan's compliment, so he repeated in English. "I said you speak Spanish very well and your accent is perfect."

"Thank you Mr.Radcliff, but I know very little Spanish except what to order in a restaurant."

"Please, call me Dan. However, I still say even people who have study the language rarely speak it like a native. Dan noticed that Mary was getting uncomfortable with his questioning, so he quickly switched to the menu. "My cooks can make any Spanish dish you like. But I must confess the ones they do best are on the menu."

Mary glanced down the menu with an experienced eye.

"If you need help, I would be glad to assist you."

"Thank you I think I can manage. Let's see now. I would like to start with *Calamares a la Roma*. And then for the main course I would like *Medallones de Solomillo.*"

Again, Dan noticed the young girl's ease with the choices. The menu he gave her had no English translations." I see you have eaten in a Spanish restaurant before.

"Yes, I love Spanish food and I have often gone to our local Spanish restaurant, *El Rincon."*

Dan's suspicion was now on full alert. This girl is more than she pretends to be, but I like a challenge, he thought. Now it was Mary's turn to ask questions:

"How do you manage to make a profit in an exclusive place like this out in the middle of nowhere?"

"I have few customers, but they spend a lot of money. After all it is an exclusive restaurant and therefore expensive. On average, I charge eighty pounds per plate.

Enough about me, I'd rather learn more about the beautiful lady in front of me. For example, why are you here in Haversay?"

"I suppose it will soon be known to all. I came because I heard my mother had died and I wanted to be at her funeral." Dan already knew this since he had a clerk on his payroll who worked in Mr. Snives office and who often gave him information that he thought would be useful to Dan.

"Did you know Maggie O'Hare?" Mary asked.

"No, I'm sorry I never knew the lady. Why didn't you come and visit her?"

Mary once again told her story, this time with less emotion than she displayed with Father Murphy.

"It must have been a shock to learn that your real mother was Maggie O'Hare. And now you are going to be rich."

"Am I? How do you know that?" She caught Dan off guard by the question.

"Well I suppose I'm guessing. It is possible. The rumour has it that she was rich and since you are her only relative, I would assume that you would get the greatest portion of the money."

"I have no idea what I'll receive. I have heard, though, that large numbers of people received invitations to the reading of the will. Have you been asked to come?"

"No, as I've said I had no dealings with your mother."

Dan snapped his fingers and two waitresses appeared. He gave them the order in Spanish. Next, a waiter appeared handing Dan a wine list.

"Do you have any particular wine that you enjoy? We also have some very good Champagne.

"I'm not a connoisseur of good wines. I would like a good dry white wine though."

"Excellente!" He then spoke to the waiter:

"Paco, por la señorita este vino blanco y trae me el Cordón."

"And where do you normally live?"

"I'm from York. I live and work there. I like to be near my parents. One of the reasons they adopted me was that they couldn't have children of their own. So I am their only child and since they are getting on I want to live near them."

"And where are you from originally?" Mary asked not wanting to be the only person giving away information.

"I came from a poor home in Battersea in London. I've worked my way out of the ghettos. It was hard work, but it was worth it." The first part was true the second part was a lie.

"I bet your parents are proud of you."

The comment surprised Dan. He hadn't thought of his parents in a long time. No, my parents wouldn't be proud of me, he thought to himself. They were honest and hard working. I only took from them.

"I'm sorry you seem upset," she said.

"It's nothing. It's just my parents are dead and every so often when I think of them I feel a bit lonely."

"How long has it been?"

"It's been only two years. But the pain is as fresh as if it was yesterday. Let's talk about something more pleasant. What did you do before you became rich?"

"I work with banks. You might say I'm one of Her Majesty bank inspectors."

Dan tried to control his expression of shock though he knew it was unsuccessful.

"Oh, I bet you really fool them. You look so young and inexperienced. And then when they try to fool you, they get caught."

"Precisely, Dan. I have been a certified accountant for six years now. The bank managers look at me and think I'm just a kid on her first job. I lull them into thinking I could be easily confused until I get a good lead. They're really shocked when they discover I am able to uncover evidence that they have been breaking the law. I wonder if this local bank here has any secrets. It seems strange to have a full-service bank in the middle of nowhere."

Dan made a great effort not to show his agitation. "Yes, I agree. I wondered the same thing myself. I do use this bank but only because it's convenient." He made a mental note to warn Biggs.

Mary enjoyed telling men of the world that she knew how to match wits with them. She could tell that Dan was nervous about the local bank. He clearly is hiding something she thought. Several times before she had seen that look, and every time she had, she soon discovered irregularities in the bank that she was inspecting.

Dan now was certain the young lady before him was a worthy adversary, that is if she chose to be. He must be more careful as to what he said. In a way though, what difference did it make. In a few months time, he would be in another country enjoying his early retirement. This latest shipment was to be his last. The asking price for it was seven million pounds. It would be a tidy sum to retire on, but then, how many times had he said that to himself? He really knew he probably couldn't stop.

While they were enjoying starters, Dan was called to the phone. He looked worried to Mary and he was. There was no reason he should be receiving a phone call just then.

As Dan left, Mary called the waiter over. "Excuse me could you tell me where the Ladies is ?"

"The waiter seemed not to understand. Mary did not have time to wait for an answer in English:

"Dónde esta los servicios para señoras?

"Hay arriba." He pointed to the second floor.

"Gracias."

"De nada, señora." It was as she had hoped it would be. Dan headed that way and she wanted to find out why he was so upset. He certainly had secrets to hide. The restaurant was just busy enough to move without being too obvious. She did see two Spanish looking men watching her as she went upstairs. She was

used to men watching her and had no idea they were Dan's bodyguards. It was a mistake she shouldn't have made.

She found the Ladies and then surreptitiously looked around to see if anyone was watching her. She then walked up a hallway clearly marked Private. She could hear Dan's voice loud and angry through the closed door of his office. She looked once more towards the way to the restaurant and put her ear to the door.

"Tenemos traer las pescas pronto. No importante sí esta lo peligroso."

It didn't make complete sense to Mary who understood Spanish perfectly. Of course, he was talking in code. He said they had to bring the fishes quickly. It wasn't important that it was dangerous. Mary was so intent on listening at the door she forgot to watch if anyone was coming. Miguel and Pedro were next to her before she could scream. Pedro's strong left hand was over her mouth with a knife in his right hand pushing against her neck. He shoved her into Dan's office.

In a different part of the village another drama was unfolding. Mrs Ruth Wright was informing Ronald her husband that she wanted a divorce. She had had enough.

Chapter 4

A BROKEN MARRIAGE

It was a dreary rainy day. Father Murphy felt restless and isolated from his work with the poor. True the pressures of his previous parish were too much for him and had cost him his health. To call his present parish quiet was an understatement. The greatest controversies were the arranging of the flowers or whether or not the congregation sing any of those 'new songs': any hymn less than thirty years old they considered as new.

Even though his previous parish was depressing and overwhelming at times, Fr Murphy felt that he was doing something valuable. Now he was here to recuperate locked away in this retirement village filled with people not wanting to die but, if averages held, would soon have no need of a parish priest. He poured himself a cup of coffee that he immediately split on his sermon notes.

"Damn, why do I have to be stuck here. How am I serving you, Lord?" Father Murphy prayed from the heart and hoped that God would understand his, sometimes, strong language. He tried to lift himself from his depressed mood by praying. He was a Catholic priest yet praying did not come easily to him. It's not that he couldn't and didn't pray it was just that he was always distracted in his prayers. As he struggled through his morning office his mind wandered and he was imagining what trouble Mary Preston might have had last night when she went to see Dan Radcliff. Though there was no proof, Father Murphy fully believed that Dan Radcliff was not an honest man. He knew of the *El Faro* restaurant yet knew of only one local couple who had ever gone there. The prices were just too high.

Ronald Wright, when he had been working, had taken his wife there for an anniversary present. The bill came to over two hundred pounds! Yes, the food and service were excellent, but who could pay such prices. He had gone into the restaurant not knowing the prices, but confident he could afford them. He was wrong. His wife, who had taken a liking to Mr. Radcliff and was influenced by his charm, thought her husband narrow minded because he complained about the bill. Their marriage was already shaky and after his employer made him redundant, the relationship went into a terminal spin.

Ronald Wright was on his mind this morning since he had a nine o'clock appointment with him to discuss his marriage. Normally he counselled both husband and wife, but Ruth Wright had no desire to mend the relationship.

Father Murphy knew that in cases like this there was little hope. He had often felt hopelessness in his counselling before. He knew in this case only a miracle would ever get them together again. The previous priest told him about Ruth Prince, which was her maiden name. It was unusual for the priest to say anything bad about any of his parishioners since he wanted Father Murphy to meet them afresh. It was just that Ruth Prince was in a category all by herself. He met her just before she had made her first Holy Communion, a spoilt brat. She was unhappy with the expensive communion dress her mother had purchased. It was too much like Alice's, her rival. She insisted that her mother purchase a prettier dress, one that would really impress everyone. A dress that would make Alice's look like rags. Unfortunately, her mother complied.

She had been an only child and her father was a well-known solicitor. Her mother and father were in their early forties when she was born and so it would have been difficult to have other children. Because her father had a good salary, they had given her what she asked for.

She had had the best private education, the latest clothes and holidays all over the world. It was a mystery why she had married Ronald. Perhaps it was because her parents had been dead set against it. After all, he was barely middleclass, and they considered themselves upper class. No, she had her excuses to remove Ronald from her life completely and no Irish priest would convince her otherwise.

"I must leave this in your hands," he finally prayed. I will concentrate on giving Ronald back his dignity, he thought, and with that, he went to have his morning cereal. When he opened the fridge, Daniel, his cat was there behind him. He did not utter a sound. The cat assumed his regal presence would be enough to jog the mind of his human keeper to get him food.

Father Michael paused for a moment wondering if Daniel would at least give him some recognition, some sign of affection rather than this demanding posturing.

"So you want to be fed do you?" Still there was no response.

"All right but just one of these days I would appreciate if you would show a bit of thanks." He took out a tin of cat food and opened it. He then produced a bowl and dutifully filled it with milk.

"Will that do your highness? Now, may your Grace allow me to eat my humble breakfast? It's plain to me you're not a Christian cat. You'll never get to heaven treating me like that I can assure you." Daniel took no notice of the ranting of his human keeper. He simply slowly ate his food as he did every day.

"Did you know in some countries they eat cats? And I hope you realise that nowhere in the Bible does it say that one must feed their cat!" With that, the dialogue ended.

Before he was half-finished with his breakfast, the phone rang. It was Mrs Biggs. She was very upset. She claimed that her husband came home and drank a whole bottle of whiskey the previous night and then left again before she got up in the morning.

"Now I would like to ask one question. If you were asleep, how did you know he drank the whole bottle in one go?"

"Well that was obvious, the bottle was empty."

"Are you sure the bottle was full last night?"

"He bought it Guy Fawkes' day. It wasn't that long ago." At this point Father Michael was tempted to tell her he had finished two bottles in that time and a third was well on its way, but though it might comfort the lady it would cause a bit of a scandal in a small village.

"I see. Did you try calling him at work?"

"I can see you don't really want to help me, Father. You think I'm making it all up." Before he could reply, she hung up the phone.

I knew this was going to be a bad day. God help poor Ronald when he comes to see me for help. He'll probably... He stopped himself before he thought the worst. The memory of the young man who he had counselled when he first became a priest was still vivid. The boy had been on drugs and was very emotionally unstable. In the end, he committed suicide. Father Michael blamed himself for his death though his friends and the Bishop had told him otherwise. He said another prayer and hoped that Ronald would leave him in a better state than on his arrival.

He had fifteen more minutes before Ronald would come. He had plenty of time to call the hotel and see if Mary Preston was all right. Before he could pick up the phone, there was a knock at the door. It was Sam the milkman coming for his money. Father Michael usually asked him in for a cup and since it was a cold and wet day, he thought he would ask him in. Sam was a good source of information. Other people more objective than Father Murphy would say he was a good source of gossip. Regardless, Father Murphy felt if he knew what the latest social behaviour in the community was, he would be in a better position to help his parishioners. It eased his conscience as he took in the latest news.

"Come on in Sam and tell me the news. I have fifteen minutes until my first appointment." Father Murphy knew that it was necessary to let Sam know that his visit had a definite time limit otherwise the rest of the community would be without their milk and he would have had a wasted day.

"I do have some exciting news. I'm working for the police now." Sam always paused to make sure his listener was really paying attention.

"And, in what way are you helping our police?" The village was so small that it only had one local constable, inappropriately called Nick, who came by on odd days of the week to let the community know that he was suitably protecting them.

"There have been burglaries in the local villages. They happen early in the morning and Nick told me to keep a sharp eye out. I've even got up earlier than usual so I could have a better chance of seeing anything that might help catch them.

"And have you seen anything unusual?"

"Not really. Nobody seems to be up before 5: 30. Even the houses are completely dark. The first light is usually above the local post office when I guess George Peterson is getting up. But there was something different this morning. There were lights on above the *El Faro*. I guess Mr. Radcliff had an early start."

"Mary..."Sorry Sam I've just remembered an important phone call I have to make."

"I haven't finished my..." Father Murphy helped a befuddled Sam out the door.

"We'll talk some other time Sam." Before poor Sam had time to turn around, he closed the door. He walked a few steps forward and turned back to look at the front door from where he had been so abruptly ejected. He shook his head and headed for his next delivery. Father Murphy dialled the number of the hotel only to get a busy signal. After five minutes, he hung up the phone in disgust. It was coffee break time and Father Mike had a feeling that a certain lazy front desk attendant purposely left the phone off the hook. The doorbell rang and Father shot up another prayer for Mary's protection.

He took a deep breath as he approached his door and looked once again for help from above. He opened the door to find a drooping Ronald. Father Murphy said hello as cheerfully as possible.

"Good morning Ronald. And how are you this day?" What a daft question, Father Murphy thought as he heard his own words.

"I'm coping," he replied in a feeble voice. It's not good for a man to feel sorry for himself. I wonder if I could convince him how lucky he would be to get rid of his selfish wife and of course not get in trouble with the Bishop.

"I was just going to have a cup of coffee. I'll make you a cup too. Have a seat and I'll be right back."

Once in the kitchen his plea for help intensified: "OK. Lord," Father Murphy prayed, "I'm not getting any ideas here. Could you please help me find a way of helping this desperate man? I don't have any ideas of my own. Thanks in advance."

After settling down in the still untidy study, Ronald began to talk. He could hardly hold his head up. "Father I'm afraid Ruth doesn't want to come back to me. She says that I am a useless failure and a dead weight."

"Is it because you don't have a job? There are thousands of men and women made redundant every year. Last year there were two thousand repossessions a month in the UK, most directly caused by the redundancy of the main earner. Are all the men and women useless just because they were made redundant? If you're neighbour was made redundant would you consider him useless?"

"Well of course not. But she..."

"What she thinks is a lot of baloney. God made us in his image and likeness and the same God died for us. It's those who treat others with less than dignity that have got it wrong!"

"I suppose I know she is wrong, but it still hurts. Maybe I could have done something to prevent me losing my job."

"Perhaps you could. Perhaps you did make mistakes. We all do. And she has no cause to blame you for everything. Perhaps she wasn't the perfect wife. Perhaps she could have supported you better.

"What I'm trying to say Ronald is that no one is perfect. We all make mistakes; we all do things wrong and we all sin. He still loves us so we must be worth something. And another thing, none of us deserves that love."

Father Murphy saw that Ronald was taking in what he said. "That same all-accepting love should be in marriages. When you married Ruth and she married you, you made a decision to love one another for better or worse. It was a decision. You didn't sign a contract that said you would stay together only if you both performed to a certain standard. Your promise to love was all accepting. That's why the statement for better or for worse is so often used. No, your dear wife has got it wrong by a long way."

"I don't know what to do though. She asked me to move out."

"What would a person who felt he was worth something do? Should you allow her to treat you with anything less than the dignity you deserve?"

"No, you're right. I wish I had the strength to stand up for myself."

"You must rely on His strength and the knowledge that you know you are right."

Ronald got up and managed a half of a smile.

"Thanks Father you've been very helpful." As he showed Ronald out the sun broke through the grey wet clouds. Thank you Lord for answering my prayers, he said quietly to himself.

As he walked back into the presbytery, he remembered Mary Preston. He nearly ran to the telephone brushing Daniel aside causing him to arch his back in alarm.

He dialled the number by memory and waited impatiently for it to ring. Finally, he heard a human voice on the end of the line.

"Ah there's life yet in the Haversay Hotel."

The response was slow but deliberate. "How can I help you?"

"For a start you can answer the phone when it's ringing. In case you haven't recognised who this is Robert, tis Father Murphy, and please, just answer my question. Is Mary Preston there in the hotel."

"Well, err I'm not sure I haven't seen her this morning." He responded more slowly than usual. He couldn't understand why Father Murphy was so agitated and this made him more nervous than he usually was and this slowed him further.

"Do you think it's possible that you could give her a ring or do I have to go over and knock at her door." Father Murphy heard his voice go up an octave as he nearly screamed in frustration into the phone.

"What, wha, what should I tell her." Father Murphy then let go completely.

"Tell her I bloody want to talk to her and quickly !!!"

"Yes, ah, yes ah right away." Father had terribly shaken Robert so much so that he hung up the phone. When Father

Murphy heard the receiver go down at the other end, he slammed down his and shouted at the top of his voice.

"That bloody idiot, how could he be so stupid!" Daniel, his cat, was fully convinced that his master was not well and at this moment, it might be dangerous to be seen by him. He shot under the table just as Father Murphy ran out of the door.

The hotel was small by any standard, ten full size rooms. It was a wooden frame structure which had stood in it present form for over sixty years. One would be generous in saying it had character when what it really needed was remodelling and modernising. At any rate, the hotel was small enough to be managed by one desk attendant and two maids and one maintenance man whose job was becoming increasingly more difficult as the building aged.

By the time he walked the four hundred metres to the hotel, he seemed to have calmed down and began to reflect on how badly behaved. He was ready to apologise to Robert as he pushed opened the hotel doors. When Robert saw him coming, he visibly froze in position. He had never known Father Murphy to be so furious. And he, like the cat, thought he might be dangerous to be around, but unlike the cat he couldn't hide.

"I'm sorry Robert. I didn't mean to be so hard on you. I just was very concerned about Miss Preston. Now, is she here?

"No, no err no." Robert was still worried for his safety.

"Did she come back last night?"

"I don't know. I could find out though." He was gaining his composure since Father Murphy was no longer shouting at him. He went off in a quick step and returned in less than three minutes slightly puffing.

"She didn't come back last night Father. Do you know what's happened to her?"

"Nothing, I hope. Thanks for your help Robert. Again I'm sorry I was so hard on you."

"That's all right Father. I'm used to it."

Father stopped to think what to do next. Mr. Radcliff was a clever man. He wouldn't reveal anything about Mary unless he was tricked into. But right then, Father Murphy was completely out of ideas and he feared he was rapidly running out of time.

Chapter 5

THE DISAPPEARANCE

Father Murphy prayed in desperation for a way to discover whereabouts Mary. She could have left the village for a while to go somewhere else. There was no reason she should tell him. As he approached his door, he saw two men, one tall and fairly well built and the other short and wiry both look very anxious to see him.

"Can I help you?" Father Murphy asked.

"Yes, I hope so. This is Detective sergeant Costello and I am Detective inspector Maxwell. We would like to have a word with you in private."

Thoughts of Mary flew from Father Murphy's head. He imagined that he would be grilled over a parishioner and would have to invoke the confidentiality of the sacrament of Reconciliation. As he opened his door, he tried to second-guess about who they would be asking and how he could put them off.

"Would you like a cup of tea or coffee? I was just going to have something myself."

"Thank you. I think we both would like a cup of coffee." Inspector Maxwell knew that if the one he was interviewing was comfortable he would get better results. As they entered the house Daniel went again into hiding. He wasn't taking any chances. He would watch and wait to see if his master had regained his senses before exposing himself to danger.

"Let me move some of these papers so you can sit down." He only had to clear one chair since he had already cleared one for Ronald that morning. He then went to pray and make the coffee. Then a frightening thought occurred to him. What if it was he they were interviewing Could someone have made a false complaint against him? Could he prove that he was innocent?

As Father Murphy came into the room with the coffee, he saw Inspector Maxwell looking over his study as if he was gathering evidence from a recent crime.

"Sorry about the mess. I'm by myself and I don't bother to clean up like I should."

"Yes, but you did have company this morning."

"Yes, in fact I had two people here. How did you know?"

"Fresh cup rings on your table. And one stack of paper taken off the chair I'm sitting on."

His examination of the room made Fr. Murphy nervous. The two visitors he had this morning were Sam the milkman and poor Ronald. Surely neither of them was the target for their investigation. Unless, oh no, could poor Ronald have killed his wife?

"Yes, I can see why you're an inspector. Ah, now what can I do for you?"

"I understand that you had a chat with Miss Preston earlier this week."

"Yes, I did."

"You see we are trying to get in touch with her on some police business and I was wondering if she said anything about her plans for today."

"Well I'll gladly tell you what I know. I'm really worried about her to tell the truth. She didn't come back from the *El Faro* last night. I know that because she didn't sleep in her bed."

"How in the devil do you know that?" The sergeant blurted out. Maxwell gave the sergeant a disapproving look.

"I went to the hotel to see her this morning. The young man who takes the bookings and answers the phone checked her room and discovered that the bed was still perfectly made."

Sergeant Costello was about to ask a further question when he decided that he had said enough. Maxwell continued his questioning.

"Could you tell us why you were concerned about the young lady's safety?"

"Yes, it's really straightforward. Dan Radcliff had invited her to the *El Faro* for dinner. I suppose there's no proof, but many think he is a criminal and certainly far more worldly than Miss Preston."

The sergeant and the inspector exchanged glances.

"That's interesting." Maxwell looked at the priest trying to discern if he knew anything more.

"There's one other small piece of information which alarmed me."

"Please tell us. Any piece of information could be helpful." Maxwell was a thorough man and carefully examined each fact he uncovered.

"The milk man, Sam List, saw a light on in Radcliff's office in the early hours of the morning. He said that this was unusual."

"I see. Can you think of anything else?"

"Can I ask you what you know about her? Did you know she was the daughter of the recently deceased Mrs O'Hare? And that in two days time she fully intended to be here to hear the reading of the will."

"Yes, we are aware of that. Do you know anything else about her?"

"No, she didn't tell me anything else. What I want to know is are you going to search Dan Radcliff's premises?"

"I'm afraid we cannot tell you what we are going to do. All I can say is I am as concerned as you are about Miss Preston and we'll do all we can to help her."

"Then you do think she's in danger?"

"It's possible."

"Well, why in the devil aren't you going to search the man's premises?"

"Father Murphy, there's nothing I dislike more than other people telling me how to do my job. Thank you for your time. I'll let you know if I need any more information."

"And will you tell me if you find her." Father Murphy was feeling his temper rising for the second time in one day. Maxwell let his question hang in the air for several moments. "Yes, of course I will. Good day sir."

Still fuming, Father Murphy showed them to the door. As he closed the door, he started thinking. The answer to why they might not storm Radcliff's premises was obvious. They were interested in getting him for something bigger and perhaps they weren't concerned about the girl's safety. Well they might not do anything, but if he could find a way perhaps, he could get some help. He couldn't rescue the girl on his own. Father Murphy was right about the need to rescue Mary. She was far beneath the ground in a cold dark room hued from stone. When Mary found herself in Radcliff's office, she knew she was in desperate trouble. Pedro had grabbed her purse and threw the contents across Radcliff's desk. In her purse was a small transmitter. No matter what she said now, it was obvious that she was working with the police.

As a bank inspector Mary often had contact with the police. If she found any serious irregularities within the Bank or in one of their customer's accounts, she would often notify them. They would assist in helping collect and impound any papers she deemed necessary which may lead to criminal charges.

Maxwell discovered by chance that Mary was going to Haversay for her mother's funeral: one of the policewomen in his unit was Mary's friend. Knowing that Mary would have the perfect cover he had asked her to help him trap Radcliff who he was certain was a drug operator. Mary had always wanted to do police work and was happy to help the Inspector. Inspector Maxwell, to his credit, did warn the girl that helping him could be dangerous. Of course, he knew that she was excited about helping capture a criminal and would give little thought to the risks involved. In addition, Mary really believed that Inspector Maxwell would protect her from any possibility of real harm. Inspector Maxwell had arranged with Mary unilaterally without his department's permission. He was desperate to catch Radcliff and when he found out that she could speak fluent Spanish, he decided to recruit her at any cost. No one would expect the grieving daughter of Maggie O'Hare to be helping the Inspector. Mary's enthusiasm for helping the Inspector had definitely waned as she found herself wondering whether she would survive the night.

"Pues Pedro y Miguel tenemos una amiga de Inspector Maxwell. Que haremos con ella?" Mary heard what they had said which was that they knew she was working with Maxwell.

Without saying another word, Radcliff gave a nod to Pedro who went to the back of the office and took something out of a cabinet. Mary wanted to turn around to see what was happening but was too frightened to move. With three strong men surrounding her, she was helpless. Again, she felt the strong hand of Pedro around her mouth. She struggled for a few moments before she lost consciousness. Pedro easily lifted the girl from her chair and carried her down a corridor that look as if it ended in a solid wall. Radcliff pulled a hidden lever that was behind a removable stone. The wall Pedro was facing began to move revealing a hidden staircase that led downward towards the beach below. This same passage had been used by smugglers hundreds of years ago.

Mary awoke feeling stiff and cold. She had no idea how long she had been unconscious. A candle dimly lit the drab cell. Alongside the candle was a box of matches. Her first attempts at getting up were painful. She could not remember when she had felt the cold so deeply. She examined the cell like room and found the walls were made of solid rock! Somewhere she heard the sound of gentle running water. There was no other sound. The quiet was absolute. Wherever she was she knew no amount of screaming would bring her help. She was sure she was deep underground and she wasn't sure if she would ever come into the light and warmth again.

Inspector Maxwell knew that Mary's life was in danger. He felt certain though that Radcliff intended to bring the drugs into Haversay by sea and he would do everything to catch Maxwell including risking Mary's life. His superintendent insisted that he was wrong. He reasoned that with the approach of a violent storm Maxwell would not bring in any drugs; it would be suicide to do so.

In fact, the Met Office had already sent out warnings that the storm would reach gale force ten. They were reluctant to ask the

Government to evacuate the western coast of the UK. Why? The UK government had never organized an evacuation before. The Chief Meteorologist had given the PM a preliminary report but played down the severity of the storm. He had nightmares that, on his word, they would evacuate the whole of the western shores of the UK: he wanted to give the PM enough information without having to make the decision.

 Of course, Maxwell did not have all this information. He, like everyone else, just knew a big storm was coming. It was doubtful that he would have believed anyone who said that the drugs wouldn't soon arrive. This was his reason for risking Mary's life.

Father Murphy though, was not waiting for Maxwell. At first, he couldn't even see how he could get into the restaurant without paying for a two -hundred- pound dinner. An idea seemed to spring from nowhere. It must be the Holy Spirit, he thought. Before he could think otherwise, he made the call that sent his plan into action. The idea was so risky that it could mean his departure from the priesthood!

Chapter 6

A FULL HOUSE

Paul Thorn, head of the Met Office, was a worried man as he looked in horror at latest information on the storm. The data on the storm was pouring in and it was alarming. Winds had reached one hundred and thirty miles an hour already and the storm's strength was growing. By conservative estimates, the storm would hit in forty-eight hours with winds up to one hundred and fifty miles per hour. If the predictions were correct, this storm would be the worst that ever hit the UK.

However, Paul Thorn had a problem. He hated making decisions. He knew he should advise the PM to evacuate the millions of people that lived on the western coast of the UK from Cornwall to northern Wales. If this was occurring in the US the procedure would be standard and no one would be upset if the storm then weakened and died offshore for such warnings had been known to save thousands of lives there. In the UK, the forecasters still claimed, as Michael Fish had told his reassured listeners in October 1987, there was no hurricane coming to the UK.

He already sent a preliminary report saying in effect that a big storm would hit the coast with winds over a hundred mile an hour. What was coming was far worse than this. He should have issued a severe storm alert for the whole country, but he feared the storm would die at sea and he would look like a fool.

He decided to send by special delivery the new update of the storm and hope the PM would act on the raw data. His assistant, Peter Tess, was incredulous at Paul's decision.

"You're not going to call him and tell him what the hell is coming. Man, in perhaps less than forty-eight hours the western coast from Wales to Land's End is going to be history and your sending him information by post!"

"If the storm dies in the sea we will be made to look like fools."

"And if it carries on the way it is going thousands may be killed. I never believed you were such an idiot."

"You'll regret those words." Peter didn't stop to answer Paul's threats. He was off to make a few phone calls before it was too late.

It wouldn't matter to Mary Preston whether or not she was there when the storm hit. She was seriously ill. The shock of her incarceration for several days without food or water had taken its toll. The temperature in the rock cell far beneath the *El Faro* was a cold six degrees Celsius. She was sinking into hypothermia and before long she would go into a coma. She lay down on her cot and curled up waiting to die.

Fr. Murphy's plan was in full swing with the help of Ronald Wright who was now receiving his final instructions: "Now I would like you to drive to Barnsley and pick up the flyers. Then I would like you to put them in all the shops and public places in Haversay. And I would like this done by four this afternoon."

"Could you tell me what these fliers say?"

"Basically, a pack of lies, but its all for a good cause."

"You want me to give out false information!"

"You might say so, yes. Ronald, its a long story and I don't have the time to answer all your questions. All I can say is a girl's life depends on you doing what I ask. I don't want you to tell anyone who asked you to do this. Do it quickly and then call me. I have a few phone calls to make myself. Please trust me. I would never have you do anything that was morally wrong."

"But it sounds like its illegal."

"Will you do it Ronald?"

"Yes, I will."

"God bless you then."

Oh, dear Holy Spirit I hope I'm reading you right. If not, my services as a priest may come swiftly to an end. He knew his next call would be the one that could easily be his ruin. He closed his eyes and sent another petition up as he lifted the receiver.

"Hello, is Bishop Cowan there? This is Father Murphy." He waited and hoped that the Bishop would be out of the country, but his precise voice answered.

"Bishop Cowan here. How can I help you Father Murphy?"

"Well I have some good news that is if you're free tonight. You know that posh restaurant *El Faro.*"

"Yes, I am acquainted with it. Why should I be interested in it? "

"I thought perhaps I could take you there for dinner tonight."

"You've won the Lottery, how nice of you to think of me."

"Well, not exactly. You see just for tonight they are offering a special, a full dinner for ten pounds which usually would cost two hundred."

"What, that's fantastic. I've always wanted to have a look inside that place. I shall drive down and be at your place at 7:30 for drinks."

"I would be delighted your Excellency."

"Until then Father Murphy. Best news I had all week."

Sweat was pouring down Father Murphy's face. Now for the second part of my plan, he thought while picking up the receiver once again to call *El Faro.*

A woman with a strong Spanish accent answered the phone. "*Hola*, this is the *El Faro,* how can I help you?"

"I would like to make a reservation for myself, Father Murphy, and Bishop Cowan for eight o'clock tonight. It's kind of a surprise party."

"Si, we have a table for two."

"Also, there will be several others phoning in from Haversay for reservations. Could you have all the people from Haversay surrounding the Bishops table? Oh, and could you also have a cake ready for us to sing happy birthday? Not a big one, just a token."

"It would have been impossible to arrange a full-size cake, but a small one we can manage."

"Could you perhaps give me an idea of how many people might be coming so we can arrange extra catering?"

"It could be as many as thirty."

"Carumba ! Hace muchas personas . That is a lot of people!"

Father Murphy didn't have a clue how many people would come. He did know that almost everyone he knew would jump at the chance of having dinner at *El Faro* but it was the prices that had stopped them. The fliers offered a one-night special price of ten pounds for a three-course dinner. He hoped that a large enough people would come to fill the restaurant. In a way, what he was asking for was a miracle.

It was six in the evening; Radcliff was in his office looking at the inflated figures of his restaurant's profits. Fake like everything about me, he thought. He then started thinking about Mary who he had locked in a cold cell three days ago. Something about her disturbed him. Why should he be so concerned about a girl who Maxwell had sent to ensure that he spent the rest of his life in prison? She reminded him of someone, but whom. In the top drawer of his desk, he kept a picture of his mother and brothers. He did not love his family, but he kept the pictures and put them out when people he wanted to convince of his integrity came by. He knew people trusted other people who cared for their family. He now took out the picture and looked at it. He carefully looked at his mother's picture and to his surprise; he could see her resemblance in the girl down below.

Now he knew who the girl looked like. It wasn't his mother. It was someone he had dearly loved and who died when he was a young man. It was his sister Marie. Her death made him curse God and filled his heart with hatred. She was young and beautiful much like the girl below. She was the only person who he felt loved him. She died of meningitis when she was nineteen years old and he sixteen. He felt the loss once again. He hated to have feelings like that. They were far too painful.

"You are a murderer," he nearly shouted at himself. He wanted no soft feeling. Yet, they would not go away. Marie's face became clearer. In his mind, he still could see those bright laughing eyes as they rode their bikes together on the common. They often had walked in the woods. She loved nature and saw

God's beauty in it as he did when he was with her. She would never forget his birthdays and her presents were ones he always cherished. She was the one who had bought him his first bike - it was a beauty. He couldn't understand why she spent a whole month's salary on a bike for her kid brother. Her reply was simply, "I like my kid brother."

Thinking about his sister unnerved Dan. Why was he thinking of her now, he asked? Yes, it was that girl down in the cell that was probably dead by now. Perhaps if he finished her off the thoughts of his sister would leave him.

He made his way through the hidden door barely closing it as he rushed towards the cell. After unlocking the door, he stopped dead. He now realised he should never have come down: she was lying on the bed almost exactly the way Marie did when she was dying. He walked over to her and felt her wrist for a pulse. To his surprise, he was relieved when he felt one. He impulsively took her in his arms and brought her upstairs. The only thing he wanted to do now was to save her life! It was as if he was experiencing a dream. Logically he knew what he was doing would put him in prison for life, but he was powerless to stop himself. Marie's life and Mary's life had become intertwined: they were one and the same. His reason for living became the saving Mary's life. He took her to his bedroom and blipped for Pedro. He kept a pager near him so he could summon his bodyguards immediately.

Pedro came to Radcliff's bedroom. He was surprised to see Mary covered and in bed, but it was his nature never to ask questions. He only did what Radcliff told him to do. Radcliff told Pedro to go to the local doctor's house and drive him back to the restaurant. As he left, he called the doctor and told him that Pedro was coming to pick him up. "Doctor Bailey, I have found a woman out near the cliffs. She must have fallen. She is very cold but alive. Please come quickly. I am sending you my car."

Having Pedro pick up the doctor gave him some kind of control of the situation. He still was amazed at his actions. He was sending himself to prison and he didn't care.

Shortly after there was a knock on the door, it was the manager of the restaurant.

"Yes, what's the problem Charles."

"Sir, we have over eighty bookings tonight. The restaurant is fully booked for the first time ever. It's just that I don't have the staff to cope. May I have permission to call in for some help?"

"Yes, of course." Radcliff was about to wave him away when he fully took in what he had said.

"Why is the restaurant fully booked tonight? By whom?"

"It seems that the local Catholic bishop is having a surprise birthday party. There's another strange thing. Inspector Maxwell and his sergeant have also booked tonight. I can't see how they can afford it or for that matter the others."

"Do you know who they are?"

"Yes, sir. They live in the village here."

"I want you to find out why everyone has booked tonight."

"Sir, may I still call in the extra help?"

"Yes, yes but find out why they are coming and let me know as soon as you do."

In London, Peter Tess was making a few important phone calls. His first call was to his mother who lived on the cost of Cornwall. His message was clear. Get out as soon as possible. There's no doubt a killer storm is coming. His parents were good people and therefore told all their neighbours. It wasn't long before large numbers of people from their village in Cornwall were leaving and they in turn were telling others. People knew that a big storm was coming; now they began to realize just how big it was. One of those who heard about it was a reporter working for the Evening Standard. He in turn tracked down a contact in the Met office that backed what he had heard. That evening the headline in The Standard read "Killer Storm Heading for West Coast."

Paul Thorn read the paper with utter horror. The word was out before he had even briefed the PM. He was at home and had just finished his resignation letter when the phone rang. His wife answered it.

"Paul, it's the Prime Minister."

He felt the cold anger of the PM as he asked him the question that he dreaded.

"Mr. Thorn. Is there truth in what I read in the paper?"

"Yes, sir there is. There will be a storm hitting us in under forty-eight hours that could have winds up to hundred and fifty miles per hour."

"Nice of you to tell me this. I suppose you were too busy watching the storm. Second question and the last one you'll be asked as head of the Met office. Should I order an evacuation of the West coast of the UK including such places as Bristol and Cardiff which substantially add to the other million people, I must ask to move out in the next forty-eight hours."

"Yes, sir. I'm afraid that's true."

"I'm not going to ask why you haven't told me this before. However, you haven't heard the last of this. If I had my way, I would hang you from the nearest tree as soon as the storm came in. Good evening Mr. Thorn."

Paul hung up the phone. The Prime Minister had given him the idea how he was to end his life. He would drive to the coast and wait for the storm that had already destroyed his life and stand in its path until it killed him.

Even as Paul put down the phone the storm's centre that was travelling at 20 knots towards shore accelerated to forty knots. Evacuation for all would be impossible.

Father Murphy had two glasses of whiskey before the Bishop arrived. He should have been fasting and praying. "The spirit is willing, but the flesh is weak," he said to himself. A few minutes later, his doorbell rang. The potential for disaster was unlimited. He saw himself before the bishop after Radcliff sued him for thousands of pounds. He could see the headlines now, 'Priest steals thousands from local restaurant.' He would be making a fool of himself and the bishop.

"Dear God, protect your foolish servant." The doorbell rang and Father Murphy walked slowly to the door as a man going to his execution.

"Good evening Murphy." The bishop never looked so happy. He didn't look like a bishop for he was dressed in an ordinary suit.

"Good evening your Excellency. I see you're in disguise tonight."

"I thought I would be less conspicuous. I don't want a lot of people knowing that I'm going to a restaurant just because the meal is going to be cheap."

"I never thought of that your Excellency. Do you want your usual drink?"

He took the Bishop's coat and looked up pleading to heaven:

"Lord," he whispered. "Please, do realise the gravity of this situation or are you telling me that I am no longer going to serve you as a priest. I needed this birthday story as a reason for the low prices. If you allow things continue on this way I will no longer be your priest."

"Are you all right Murphy? It looks as if you're talking to my coat."

"Actually, I was just having a word with the Man. I'll get your drink now."

It was seven when the Bishop and Father Murphy set off for the restaurant. The third whiskey Father Murphy drank was just enough to hold down his nerves. He hoped that few people took up the flyer's offer. Everyone knew the bishop no matter how he was dressed, and they would all want to say hello. Father Murphy just remembered the cake. How in the world would he explain that to the bishop? And all this was to rescue Mary who he only thought was hidden somewhere nearby He obviously hadn't thought this one through.

At that moment the manager of the restaurant called a Mrs Thomas, a pensioner, who lived in the same bed and breakfast as he did. She told him about the flyer offering the special deal. After that it didn't take him long to track down the man who printed them. Unfortunately, the printer knew Ronald Wright. The manager was at that moment bringing this incriminating evidence to Mr. Radcliff.

Chapter 7

THE LAST SUPPER

As Father Murphy and the bishop left the presbytery, the winds were blowing with near gale force.

"I thought we had forty-eight hours before this storm was hitting. I can't see the winds blowing with much more force than they are now." The roaring wind prevented Father Murphy from hearing him.

"The paper said that it was a killer storm coming which could have winds up to two hundred miles per hour," replied Father Murphy. He was happy to be thinking of another danger not of his making. After all, it would be far nobler for him to meet his demise through the killer storm rather than the Bishop strangling him.

"You can't believe the newspapers, Father Murphy. If the story was true, then why isn't the government doing anything? It would be totally irresponsible for it to just stand by and let it happen."

"Perhaps it would be bad for business to evacuate half of the U.K.," replied Father Murphy, anxious to keep the Bishop's mind occupied.

When they arrived, they found the restaurant's car park nearly full. There'll be quite an audience for my defrocking thought Father Murphy. The waiters and waitresses seemed to be running everywhere. All the tables were full except one right in the centre of the main room. As the astonished Bishop made his way to his table, almost everyone greeted him.

"Good evening Bishop, many happy returns."

The Bishop smiled sheepishly and after the waitress seated them and gave them menus, he turned towards Father Murphy and whispered: "What in the blazes is going on here Murphy? Why are all these people wishing me a happy birthday?"

"I'm really not quite sure Bishop. Shall we order?" The Bishop looked suspiciously at Father Murphy then turned towards his menu.

"I can't make head or tail of this menu, Murphy. What does it mean? It's all in Spanish."

Father Murphy took out a folded piece of paper from his pocket. "I think you'll find this helpful."

He handed the Bishop the same menu written in English.

"How did you get this Murphy?"

"One of the waiters goes to our church. I asked him to write down the menu months ago since I was curious what they were serving here."

"I see what I want. I'm going to have the grilled scotch fillet steak. It will be a miracle if they can produce that for ten pounds."

"An excellent choice." Father Murphy momentarily had forgotten why he was there when he saw the menu. Food was his biggest weakness and now he was madly salivating as he gazed down at all the possibilities the menu offered.

"It all looks so good. I can't make up my mind. I'm afraid I'm having the same as you. I would just be coveting your steak if I took something else."

"Yes, I suppose coveting your Bishop's steak would be a serious sin." The Bishop seemed happy for the moment, so Father Murphy looked around to see who was there. In a table close by was Ronald Wright with two other men. He wasn't with his wife. It seemed most of the village was there from Mr. Snives the solicitor to Sam the Milkman. Most of the tables were composed of couples. Even Veronica Stillwater was there with her favourite gossip partner Mrs. Penelope Barnes. If I manage to embarrass the Bishop, this might turn out to be Veronica's best night, Father Murphy thought.

The headwaiter, who seemed under a lot of strain, came up to the Bishop and Father Murphy.

"I am sorry Señors I haven't been able to take your orders. We are so busy tonight, but I am now ready." Both men looked at the mouth-watering menu hoping that their steaks would still be available.

"I think we both are having the grilled scotch sirloin if that is possible," the Bishop looked up hopefully for a positive response. "*Dos entrecotes a la plancha*", the waiter mumbled to himself as he scribbled on his order pad. "I will let you know if there are any difficulties señors" He walked quickly to the kitchen.

"Please God, let them have some steak left," prayed Father Murphy.

'"Amen", added the Bishop. On their table was a bottle of wine so time moved happily and quickly for the two men. Father Murphy saw Ronald Wright along with a friend on one of the back tables. Ronald seemed happy enough which meant that the management had not yet discovered the reasons why all these people were here.

"I heard that you gave quite a sermon the other day at widow O'Hare's funeral."

Father Murphy wondered how the Bishop found out. The usual way that the Bishop found out about a sermon was that someone complained.

"Miss Veronica Stillwater wrote me a revealing letter. She said you as much as implied that she was a gossip from the pulpit when you looked directly at her when you were referring to those who maligned the widow's reputation. She implied further that you saw Maggie O'Hare by yourself and perhaps I should look into the matter."

"I do admit to the fact that I was looking at her. It was people like her that made Maggie O'Hare become a recluse."

"I think you are absolutely right. Father Malvern, your predecessor, informed me of her activities within the first week he arrived in the parish. I replied to the letter saying that I was sure Father Murphy wasn't referring to you but sometimes the Holy Spirit illuminates one's sins and perhaps there was truth in what you thought he implied."

"And how did you respond to her accusations that I was visiting Maggie for reasons other than the salvation of her soul?"

"Well Father Murphy how do I know what went on between you and Maggie. Of course, I'm kidding, but I had the unholy urge to say that our priest are under a lot of strain and what harm would it do for them to experience a little human pleasure."

"Bishop, I'm shocked."

"I bet you are," laughed the bishop. "And here are our steaks!"

A contented gaze covered Father Murphy's eyes, as he tasted his grilled sirloin. They had prepared it perfectly. He was about to ask the Bishop if he thought steaks would be eaten in heaven when he noticed that Inspector Maxwell and his sergeant were also present. He wondered if they were planning to search for Mary. That they were there gave him false hope. For the Inspector would do nothing to jeopardise his chances of getting his hands on the drugs, which he was sure, would soon arrive. In fact, at that moment, the sergeant and the Inspector were having a difference of opinion over this point.

"What are we going to do about Mary, Inspector? Are we going to sit here while she is slowly tortured?"

"Don't be stupid, he wouldn't torture her. He's just holding her in safe keeping until the drugs are delivered."

"You're pretty damn sure of that or are you just worried that it would mess up your case against Radcliff if we attempted to help her?"

"Sergeant I am becoming more and more exasperated with you telling me I'm not doing my job. If you don't want to go back to walking the beat and giving parking tickets, I suggest you shut up!" The Sergeant restrained himself from walking out.

As Father Murphy and the Bishop finished their steak, Fr. Murphy suddenly remembered about the birthday cake he ordered. I'll soon be undone he thought. Perhaps I could get them to cancel it. Tell them it would be too embarrassing for the Bishop.

He had no idea how embarrassing it was going to be. The traditional way that a cake was presented at the *El Faro* was by a single pretty senorita that would bring in a cake and then present herself! The form this presentation was the subject of discussion between the manager of the restaurant and the girl, Margarita, who was to do it.

Margarita came from a small village in Spain called Pinoso west of Alicante. She came from a poor family and had no prospects of breaking out of her poverty. She spent a brief time in Madrid where she hoped someone would discover her talents as a dancer. She ended up in a low- class club as a flamenco dancer where she finished the dance topless. It was there that Dan Radcliff found her. He offered her a chance to become a dancer in England but for the last six months, all she was doing was a Spanish version of a strip-o-gram for special clientele who came to the restaurant. She was in the country illegally and she knew if she crossed Mr. Radcliff, he would have her deported in disgrace.

The evening's events angered Charles Evans, the manager of the restaurant, who knew Mr. Radcliff would hold him responsible for the thousands of pounds that would be lost that night because someone had advertised that the meals would only cost ten pounds. He was determined to provide an excellent meal for all to the highest standards, but he would have his revenge. It was obviously someone working for the Bishop had arranged this party at the restaurant's expense. In addition, he was determined it was the Bishop who would pay.

"Señor Evans I do not want to strip in front of the Bishop. It wouldn't be right."

"If Mr. Radcliff finds out you are refusing my request he will phone the authorities."

In reality, he would do no such thing since he also was breaking the law by hiring an illegal immigrant, but Margarita was used to bullies intimidating her and she thought she had no choice.

"I can no go back. I be dishonoured. I do it."

As Margarita was preparing for her performance Dr. Bailey had arrived to examine Mary Preston. The doctor was a tall distinguished looking man who came to Haversay for early retirement. He had been there for eight years and knew everyone in the small village. He was a kind gentle man but one who understood human nature and he well understood Dan Radcliff and did not like him or trust him in the least. Mr. Radcliff came to meet the doctor himself.

"Thank you for coming so quickly doctor." Dr. Bailey looked at Dan Radcliff with open distaste. He had examined the previous bank manager who had allegedly fallen off a cliff one dark night after an argument with Radcliff.

"Where is this woman whom you found in the night?"

"She is in my own bed." Radcliff led him to Mary. The doctor followed Radcliff without saying a word. He found the girl covered with a warm blanket, but she was as white as any patient he had ever seen. He searched for a pulse and eventually found a weak one. He did not even need to be a doctor to see the woman was suffering from hypothermia.

He looked straight at Radcliff and asked, "What is the woman's name?" The directness of the question had taken Radcliff by surprise. As if resigned to his fate Radcliff responded truthfully.

"Her name is Mary Preston the daughter of the recently deceased Maggie O'Hare."

Dr. Bailey took out a black notebook and recorded her name. In fact, he could have easily remembered it but he was making it clear to Radcliff that an investigation would take place.

"She must be sent to the hospital in Beer. I don't think she has much of a chance and time is of the essence. May I use your phone?"

"Yes, of course." He picked up the receiver and then turned to Radcliff.

"After I make this phone call, I'll let you call the police. They'll need to have a statement from you."

"Hello, Dr. Bailey here in Haversay at the *El Faro*. Could you send an ambulance here as quickly as possible? I have a patient who has severe hypothermia. I'll do what I can before you arrive."

He hung up the phone looking worried. "They'll try to come, but they are concerned about the storm. Several roads are already closed. Can you have some hot water bottles heated up and can you perhaps find some more blankets. Her body temperature must be increased if she is to live."

"Of course, I'll do that immediately."

Twenty minutes later, the waiters were serving the sweets to the waiting villagers. Without warning, a large branch from a tree struck the main window overlooking the sea cracking it from top to bottom. Three tables of people left the feast in fear of their safety. They left the advertised price of the meal plus five- pound tips that they assumed generous. At the same time, those remaining in the restaurant could hear the siren of the approaching ambulance. The room instantly stilled. The roar from the storm and the whistling of the wind through the cracked window were the only sounds heard.

. Charles now had Ronald's name and he told two of his biggest waiters not to allow him to leave until he talked to him.

Sergeant Costello observed the events grimly.

"You know damn well nothing is going to happen tonight. I'm going and I'm going over your head on this one. I don't give a damn what happens. I'll not stand by and see a human sacrificed for your success!"

"You're finished Costello," replied the Inspector vehemently. Costello did not reply. He left the room without paying for his meal. He knew he was finished but he did not care.

Father Murphy noticed that the Inspector and the sergeant were arguing, and he once again reminded himself of why he was here. He must act soon.

"That was delicious, Father. I'm glad you brought me here tonight though I am getting worried about the storm. Shall we have our sweet and leave?"

When Father Murphy heard the word leave, he began to panic. Before he could move, he saw the catalyst that launched him into decisive action. Pedro was at Ronald's table asking him to come with him. The game was up, and Father found himself on his feet.

"What the devil are you doing man?" asked the Bishop.

"I have to go to the loo and quickly." Father headed towards the men's not sure where next he would turn. As he got up, he passed the headwaiter.

"Padre, shall we give the Bishop his cake now?"

"Yes, of course. Now is the time." Father thought at the time the distraction of the cake would give him the opportunity to have a good look around. If distraction was what he was looking for then his timing was excellent. However, if he fully realised what he was authorising he certainly would have never said yes.

Inspector Maxwell received an urgent message on his phone, the local police were on their way to investigate the finding of a woman by Dan Radcliff:

"Inspector Maxwell, we have just received a message about a woman found by Radcliff who is in critical condition. We thought we would inform you that we are coming and of course we would be happy for you to be there when we interview him."

"I would request that you don't come."

"We have to. We've been called and as far as we know this is a local incident. Our superintendent requested that we go, but to respectfully notify you."

"I guess I have no choice then." Maxwell shut off his mobile thinking how he could rescue the situation.

Father could hear the strains of happy birthday and then he heard music that he knew doomed him as a priest. The sound of provocative music told father that the Bishop was getting something besides a cake.

As he headed towards Maxwell's office one of the staff, who was keeping an open way so that ambulance men could take away Mary, stopped him. He was stunned when he saw them carry her out. He knew he was too late, and all his complex plans were useless. He lost his priesthood for nothing!

He went back into the dining room and was surprised to hear two policemen addressing the diners:

"We have come here on other business, but we have been notified through official channels that everyone within fifty miles of the coast should move inland to safety. There is an extremely dangerous storm headed this way. Everyone must evacuate from the coast. There will be storm shelters put up in various towns. You are advised to tune to channel 1000.9 FM on your radios which is the UK Classical Radio station for further instruction."

People at first got up from the tables slowly but in less than a minute the panic rush for the door began: the full horror of the message hit them. The killer storm was licking at their heels. This time the headlines in the newspapers were correct!

Father went to the Bishop as quickly as he could. He began to apologise to the Bishop.

"Bishop I'm terribly sorry for what happened this evening. I will take full responsibility."

"For what man! It was one of the best nights of my life. But I would be pleased if you could drive us inland so I can live a few more moments with the memories of this evening."

"Yes of course."

The storm's power was beginning to land on the shores of England as winds up to hundred miles an hour roared down upon those who were unfortunate enough to be still near the sea. Out at sea a huge wave was rushing inland fired by the storms high wind and the Spring Tide. Haversay had only hours left as a village!

Chapter 8

THE STORM STRIKES

The Met Office had forecasted that the full force of the storm would hit in twenty-four hours. Winds were already gusting at well over hundred miles per hour. The government commandeered all the television stations to warn those within twenty miles of the western shores of the England, and to give them information on the evacuation procedures. They hoped that the storm would lose some of its strength over land. Weather experts had warned that there might be accompanying tornadoes with the storm and those who had houses on reasonably high ground and had cellars should prepare to stay in them until the storm passed.

Staying in a cellar might save lives if one lived twenty miles inland. Those who lived near the sea who hid in cellars might well drown. This was the situation in Haversay and the people there who were deciding whether or not to stay or go were deciding if they would live or die!

The government was doing all it could to move the people away. The major cities, like Bristol and Cardiff, had the army, local police as well as the local emergency services helping in the evacuation. Time was short and for a small village like Haversay the people would have to shift for themselves.

Paul Thorne checked the latest information on the storm and headed for Haversay where he knew the storm's centre would hit. He parked his car in the *El Faro's* parking lot and walked down the twenty-foot drop to the rocky beach below. The wind screamed as it struck the low cliffs behind him. The sea heaved millions of tons of water against the solid rocks. Paul stared straight ahead at the storm shaking his fists at it, taunting it to destroy him. The black and green sea was hardly distinguishable from the black and green clouds pouring rain above it. Both the sea and the sky had an alliance of destruction and Paul was asking to be its first victim. He couldn't face the responsibility of what he had done. If the storm abated, then he could perhaps go back and live a semblance of life he had before. Paul did not think of his wife or two married children. He had decided to end his life. He thought it was his right since it was his body. He didn't see the thirty-foot wave that threw him against the rock wall crushing his body beyond recognition.

The ambulance carrying Mary Preston took the coastal road to Beer. The wind and rain made the trip nearly impossible. The road stayed clear mainly because there were few trees near it. The winds were now gusting up to hundred and ten miles an hour, which often threw the ambulance off the road. The medics were very thankful to reach the hospital. They brought Mary into the hospital and decided to weather the storm there. The hospital had thick-stone walls and the seaward side was protected by a rock formation about fifteen feet high.

The winds over Cardiff and Bristol were now gusting at hundred and twenty miles an hour. It was dangerous to be out in these winds. The only thing that drove people out was the threat of winds well over hundred and sixty miles an hour. Unfortunately, the winds were already throwing power lines, tiles and trees across the roads bringing traffic to a halt. It was becoming horribly apparent that the evacuation had started too late and that the people who were now moving slowly out of the big cities were at risk. With the falling of power lines came the dreaded black out. Those trapped on the blocked roads waited helplessly as the storm built up its power for destruction.

The awaited nightmare for some struck without warning. A tornado touched down and moved along two miles of the slow - moving traffic on the M4 lifting and tossing hundreds of cars like they were pieces of paper. In one of the cars was Samuel Adams a professional car thief. He had just stolen the car he was driving, a new Volvo. He felt the car lifting hundreds of feet above the ground while violently twisting and shaking. He watched in fear and amazement as roofs, trucks and other cars floated by. When he realised that he was going to die he prayed for forgiveness. The tornado that was twisting the car he was in was like his life, out of control. The tornado dropped his car over a grove of young pine trees which had broken the fall enough so that he survived. The man's repentance was real. He never would steal another car again. Some others were not as fortunate as he was. Most died instantly.

The winds roared over Haversay as Fr. Murphy and the Bishop came to the presbytery. They went in just long enough to get the keys for the car. The wind began to roar and the whole presbytery shook, windows broke, and furniture began to fly about the house. The blast only lasted a few minutes and ended with a large crash just outside the door. The latest onslaught from the storm had cut all electric power to Haversay. Fr. Murphy found a torch and he and the Bishop carefully went to their cars. When they walked out the wind had momentarily stopped. They then saw the cause of the crash that they had heard: a large oak tree crushed Both Fr. Murphy's car and the Bishops'. They stood a few moments in silence.

"Well it appears that the Lord has cut off our retreat Father. What shall we do?"

"The church has a cellar. That will probably be as safe and dry as anywhere. I'll go in and get some blankets and pillows. I think it will be a long night."

The police car taking Dan to Beer left about fifteen minutes after the ambulance. Dan watched the storm impassively. He was thinking of his sister and how much she loved him. He wondered how he could have ever forgotten. He hoped that somehow, she never found out all the awful things that he had done. He also thought of his parents who had and probably still did love him. They always sent him a birthday card with a little cheque and another card at Christmas. They had stopped asking him to come visit. He was sorry now that he had treated them so badly. Perhaps they would visit him in prison.

The accident happened very quickly: the driver of the car saw a tree in front of them too late after they turned a bend in the road. Swerving to avoid colliding with the tree, he miscalculated, and the car with the passengers fell off the road into the ocean below. Dan would have no visitors in prison.

Mrs Wright left with her two daughters leaving behind Ronald who was busy looking after some of the elderly people who had no way of getting out of Haversay. He couldn't get anyone of them to leave their homes, and understandably so, since now it was obvious that it was too dangerous to be riding in a car. He had helped several though into their cellars where they perhaps could survive the storm. One of the houses he called on was that of the two spinsters, Miss Veronica Stillwater and Penelope Barnes.

He banged on their door for quite awhile before anyone answered.

"Oh, it's you Mr. Wright. Come in, you really shouldn't be out in the weather like this."

"I come to warn you that you really should leave if you can. I know the storm is bad now, but they say it will get even worse."

"Thank you for your concern Mr. Wright but Penelope and I have decided to stay here regardless of the dangers. After all, we know what people are like and if the storm breaks our windows or blows off our roof then after the storm people would come to steal our things. We know that happens. We've seen it on television in the United States. However, they have police there to protect property. Here we have one useless constable."

"Do you have a cellar then? If you're staying it would probably be the safest place."

"No we don't so if you don't mind we are just about ready to have our evening tea. Good night."

Ronald left with a clear conscience. He did his best. They were more concerned with their possessions than their lives. Just before they had their tea, the lights went out. Unperturbed they lit candles and made the decision to go to bed downstairs where they had moved their sleeping things.

"Can you imagine if we left our dear old grandfather clock, our china and crystal: they would all disappear? That would really be a shame."

"Your right as usual, Veronica. I wouldn't have put it past Mr. Wright to be in here in a flash after we left to gather up what he could. After all we know he has nothing and is nothing."

"Of course, you're absolutely right Penelope. I'm glad we have decided to stay."

Twenty miles west of Haversay Mrs Wright and her two daughters, Margaret and Hazel, had nearly reached safety. They had heard on the radio that Leedtown had a shelter in a large storage cellar that was large enough for several hundred people.

"Mum, shouldn't we have waited for Dad. He may not make it in time," remarked a slightly concerned Hazel.

"I did all I could to convince your father that he should come with us. He decided to stay and be the hero." Actually, when Ronald told her he was staying she said that it was just as well since she would have more room in the car for her things.

"Dad probably needs to help other people. He couldn't help himself could he mother?"

"Well you're probably right there. At least he feels needed. A man needs some kind of job."

She thought to herself. He's no good to me if he can't make any money. Perhaps the storm will solve one of my biggest problems. She was dreaming about how nice it would be to be free of Ronald when a tree fell only fifty feet in front of the car. There was no time to stop. The car crashed into the tree and another tree alongside the first fell on to of what was left of the car. Mrs Ruth Wright's last thoughts were not ones that a person would choose to take with them into eternity.

Ronald Wright was at that moment driving out of Haversay having tried to warn as many people as he could. He was heading towards Leedtown where he knew his family had headed. The winds were now gusting up to hundred and thirty miles per hour. As he was approaching the high ground near the top of Haversay Valley, he saw that a tree was blocking the road. He knew he was trapped. However, a thought came to him. There was a small cave not far from the road. It would be cold, but it certainly would be a perfectly safe place to shelter from the high winds of the storm.

He got out of the car and was about to turn out his lights when he saw bright reflection from the midst of the fallen tree. It was a car, one he was sure he recognised. The wind was so strong he had a hard time standing. A large branch flew over his head nearly hitting him. He was torn between running to the cave or seeing what or who was under the tree. Perhaps someone needed help. As he came closer, he saw it was Mr. Biggs' car, the man who repossessed his house. Headlights from the car guided him as he made his way deep within the tangles of the tree. Mr. Biggs was in the car his head bleeding and unconscious. Ronald worked his way around to the driver's side as a fierce gust of wind nearly lifted the tree off the ground knocking him down. He knew he was risking his life to help a man who destroyed him, but he could let him die in the car without doing all he could to save him.

He once again made it to the driver's side and was able to drag Mr. Biggs out of the car. He still had a four-hundred-yard walk to the cave. It was a cave, which had had many visitors and even, it was rumoured, several wild parties, so the path to the cave was wide and easy to follow. When Ronald finally made it, he collapsed from exhaustion. The gusts of wind now had reached hundred and forty miles an hour ripping the roofs off houses. It was impossible for anyone to survive in the open, even bricks were flying through the air making deadly missiles. It wasn't long before the walls of houses were collapsing, and Penelope and Veronica were then wishing that they had left with Ronald Wright.

Inside the room where they had held Mary Preston prisoner were Pedro, Miguel Charles and Margarita hoping that the solid rock walls would protect them from the freak storm. They had a portable radio and were listening to the news of the progress of the storm. The winds now reached well beyond hurricane force and the instruction were to stay indoors no matter where you where located. Though the storm held them prisoner, they felt safe even with the knowledge that it was centred over Haversay.

"Is safe here Charles," asked Margarita?

"Yes, I am sure no storm could knock through these walls. They're over twenty feet thick." Nevertheless, when he heard the wind whistling through the tunnel, he was not so sure. Pedro and Miguel sat stoically waiting for the storm to pass. They had no idea how bad it really was. Charles listened intently to the news. He wasn't interested in how fast the winds were blowing, but rather how high the seas were. Of course, it would be impossible for anyone to get that information directly though perhaps one could infer how high it was by how many and what roads were closed due to flooding. Charles calculated that the room they were in was about forty feet above the normal sea level. Then the sea wasn't presently normal. He would never hear this information. For now, the high spring tide and the strong westerly winds had created a massive tidal wave that was thundering towards Haversay.

Above the cave, the inspector was still sitting in the restaurant drinking himself into a stupor. He knew that he had lost Dan Radcliff and had sacrificed Mary Preston for nothing. What he had done was stupid. More than anything though, he felt Radcliff had outsmarted him once again. His hatred for the man was intense. He was even imagining how he might kill him when the tidal wave smashed through the restaurant. The restaurant was above the cell holding the three men and one woman. Everyone there was now under water.

The weather satellite had picked up the tidal wave, which hit the western coast of the UK. It rushed as much as ten miles inland destroying everything in its wake. Haversay itself, what was left of it, was completely under water. There were no survivors in the village itself. The only survivors near were the three people who had sought the safety in a small cave above the village.

Chapter 9

THE THREE SURVIVORS

The storm had spent its fury by early the next morning. All that remained was a grey sky and a steady but light drizzle. The damage it had done was equal to the bombing of England during World War II. It had destroyed most of the infrastructure of Cardiff and Bristol. Severe damage went as far North as Liverpool. There was no electricity for half the country. The damage to England was such that the International Red Cross was sending all available resources to its aide.

Ronald Wright woke up cold, stiff and sore but happy to be alive. He listened to the quiet of the morning. The only sound he could hear was the running of water towards the settling sea. Ronald gently shook Peter Biggs whose ashen face indicated the need for urgent medical help. As Peter was coming to, the sound of someone coughing from the back of the cave startled Ronald. He had though Peter and he were the only ones who had sought shelter there.

He looked back into the dark greyness and saw the form of a man moving painfully slow towards him. When the man came into the greyness of the morning Ronald could see that it was Mr. Snives.

"Mr. Snives. How long have you been in the cave?"

"I must have arrived after you did. I was trying to drive out from Haversay, and I came across your car and of course the tree. The wind was nearly lifting my car off the ground, so I crawled towards the cave. The wind was so strong I was afraid to stand up. It's a good thing I stayed crawling because a roof from a house sailed over my head and crashed into the side of this hill. I crawled to the back of the cave and vaguely remembering seeing you two."

Mud covered Mr. Snives and he had several small cuts and bruises. He was in a terrible state: his coat and trousers were torn; his face was drawn and pale; he was limping ,and his right hand was shaking. Ronald now had two people he had to care for and he himself was not in the best of shape.

Peter Biggs had finally opened his eyes. He tried to sit up but couldn't.

"Do you want some help?" asked Ronald.

"How very kind of you," he croaked and held out his hand. Ronald propped him up against a nearby rock.

"How did I get here?" he asked in a weak voice.

"I found you in your car last night trapped under a tree. I pulled you out and brought you here. Mr. Snives here came in after us."

"Ah yes, I vaguely remember a tree in the road. I couldn't stop in time and after that I have no memories. The storm, it was the worse thing I have ever experienced. I wonder how badly the storm has damaged the village."

"I thought I might have a look around and see if I can find some food and water. And perhaps I could get Doctor Bailey to have a good look at you two," said Ronald.

"You don't look so good yourself," laughed Mr. Snives.

"I'll be back in about ten or fifteen minutes." Ronald left and made his way down towards Haversay that was less than a mile from where they were. He had to walk carefully because of the debris and the running water, which was sometimes several feet deep. He came to a vantage point where he thought he would be able to see the village. He first had to climb over a very large cedar tree blocking the way. When he finally completed the climb, he stood in shock as he saw what was left of Haversay: not one house had a roof. In some cases where he thought houses should have been, all that remained were gaping holes. It reminded him of pictures he had seen in other places; America, Bangladesh, places that were used to terrible storms. He decided he couldn't face looking through the village on his own. He was sure that underneath all the rubble there would be bodies. No, he would go back for the others. Maybe together, the three of them could search the village. Ronald thought if Haversay was this bad other villages may be equally damaged and perhaps possibly worse. As for Dr. Bailey, if he had stayed in Haversay, he wouldn't be helping anyone again.

Ronald approached the cave physically and emotionally exhausted. Just before he did, he noticed a large cardboard box that appeared to have blown from one of the village stores. He picked it up and found it was quite light. It contained boxes of cereal. At least he didn't come back empty handed.

"Well done Ronald," greeted Mr. Snives when he saw that he was carrying food. "We'll have to make sure we try to find the owner."

Ronald didn't reply to Mr. Snives comment. He was sure the owner of the box was no longer on this earth. After the three had eaten, Ronald decided to tell them what he had seen.

"If you two are up to it I would like you to walk with me down to Haversay. But before you go, I would like to warn you that the village doesn't exist anymore."

"What do you mean it doesn't exist," challenged Peter.

"I mean to say, Peter, that there is not a single house standing. The storm has levelled all the homes and businesses. I'm asking you to come with me since I don't want to go there on my own."

"Oh, my God!" responded Peter.

"If what you say is true, Ronald. I can't see how there is a God. How could a so-called loving God let our whole village be destroyed? There had to be many innocent people living there," challenged Mr. Snives.

"I don't know the answer to your question, Mr. Snives. I do know that the same thing has happened in other countries. Why is it that England is so special?"

"Well, it never happened here before. I can't believe that Haversay no longer exists. However, I'll go with you. I'd like to see the village where I have spent the last thirty years of my life."

"How are you Peter? Are you up to a short walk?"

"Yes, and I hope to find the bank completely destroyed along with *El Faro* and anything else that, that bastard Dan Radcliff owned. I really was his prisoner and I hope I am free now."

"You would have probably been free of him anyway. The police took him away early last night. He's probably safe in jail or dead."

"Well I'll be damned. It's amazing how life can change in such a short time. My greatest problem vanished in one night. Though if what you say is true, we all have a few more problems to deal with."

Since Peter was the one who needed the most help Mr. Snives supported him on one side by Ronald and on the other side. The three men left to survey what was left of their village. They reached the point where Ronald had overlooked the devastation of the village.

"Oh my God," was Peter's response when he saw the destruction. "To think that we lived in this village thinking that life would go on its way. Who could have ever imagined this."

Mr. Snives looked over the remains in a dream-like state.

"All I had was in the village, thirty years of working and living. In all that time, I had never thought about why I was doing what I did. I just did my job. Now I can see the futility of the whole thing. My living and other peoples' lives blown out like a candle. What does it all mean?"

Ronald then spoke. "My life was smashed before the storm ever hit. I have already lost my wife and two daughters. I think she would have been pleased to know that I have died."

"You don't really know that Ronald," responded Peter. "Families are always having disagreements. It doesn't mean they'll split."

"Mr. Snives knows differently. He was processing our divorce."

Mr. Snives turned toward Ronald and shook his head: "Dear boy, your wife was not the finest human in the world. She wouldn't have been satisfied with anyone. You're better off without her."

Ronald smiled. "Yes, I know that, yet she is my wife and I always will think of her as such. If you both are all right, I would like to carry on. It looks like we might get some more rain and I don't feel like getting any wetter."

At the highest point in the village was the church. Even so, the wind and the sea had torn it down. The three men viewed the destruction in silence. Ronald recognised the battered remains of the Bishop's car and Fr. Murphy's car. Fifty feet away from the cars was a hole filled with water, which was all that was left of the church and presbytery.

"So the holy men have met their master," commented Snives.

"All those stories they told pretending to know what they were talking about. I wonder if heaven and hell is as if they described it." Mr. Snives had quit going to a church of any kind since he was eight. His experience of church was of a minister trying to convince a congregation how sinful they were and how God would punish them for every sin they ever committed if they did not repent. For Mr. Snives, God was a God of vengeance.

"Did you ever hear one of Fr. Murphy's sermons? "

"Are you kidding? Me go into a church, a Catholic Church."

"Then you have no idea what he said or what he believed."

"I think I've heard it all before. Besides in view of what you see before you, you have to admit it's all a bit of a joke."

"Yes, it would be if death is the end. St. Paul said that himself. ' If only for this life we have hope in Christ, we are to be pitied more than all men.' But millions of Christians believe that there is life after death."

"Gentlemen, I don't think this it the time to have arguments about religion," interrupted Peter. "Let's have a look at the bank which enslaved me." The bank was lower down into the village towards the sea. The buildings were so thoroughly demolished that it was difficult to even find the High Street.

"Is it possible what I am seeing? Has the centre of our village been washed completely away?" Peter shook his head. The other two men also saw the massive gorge, which now cut the village in half. It went straight through what was the bank.

"It looks as if my responsibility to my creditors is left solely with the insurers. The bank no longer exits." All three men stared into the gorge. Deep down in the centre was a large black box.

"I'm sorry Peter you still have a little job to do. Unless my eyes deceive me the safe is down there waiting for you to hall it out."

"Not I, I've just retired."

"Let's look and see what's on the other side of this ghastly gorge." Ronald knew that his house and that of Peter's lay somewhere among the ruins. The three men first came to what was left of Ronald's house. They stood silently in front of it.

"Ronald before you say anything, I would like to apologise for insisting that you move out of your home. I had no call to do that, not on moral grounds. I wasn't blinded to your suffering. Once I made that stupid decision, I felt awful. I tried to justify it on business grounds, but there is no justification for throwing any one out of their home. Forgive me Ronald." Mr. Biggs lowered his head.

"I accept your apology. In light of this mess it doesn't seem that important."

"Did your family leave in time Ronald?" asked Mr. Snives.

"Well, they did leave before things got terribly bad. I was heading towards Leedtown when the tree stopped me. I pray they are safe." Ronald saw a few of his things scattered about. He found a torch that worked when he turned it on and then under a board, he found a picture of his wife and two children. He picked it up and put it in his pocket with a sigh.

They continued to walk in silence. The absolute devastation of the village was overpowering. Peter then came to where his home should have been. He looked up and down and around, but he wasn't sure he was in the correct place.

"I don't know gentlemen. I think my home should have been somewhere here. I'm just not sure. How can one tell when all that is left is rubble? I pray my family made it to safety. Please God." Poor Mr. Biggs began to cry. The shock of losing so much and the thought of losing his family too were unbearable.

"When did they leave?"

"Oh, they left in plenty of time, a good two days ago. My wife believed the rag papers. I told her they printed a lot of nonsense. She said it wouldn't hurt to be safe, so she went to stay with her brother in Epsom."

"Cheer up man. She would have to be safe there," said Ronald. The three walked a bit further when a large grandfather clock caught Ronald's eye.

"You see that clock. It belongs to Veronica Stillwater and Penelope Barnes. I think they would be mortified to learn that it was out in the open for anyone to take. They wouldn't leave their home. They were afraid that someone would steal their things. Now it looks like it won't make any difference to them."

"I'd like to share something with you gentlemen. Normally to talk about some one's will before the reading would be illegal and unethical. But things aren't normal. Veronica was to be given three thousand pounds from Maggie O'Hare's estate. However, there were conditions, which were quite unusual. In order to obtain the money Veronica would have to apologise for spreading vicious lies about Maggie before a full Sunday congregation.

When I read that, I did laugh. Can you imagine our village's biggest gossip admitting that she was just that? I'm sure she wouldn't have admitted to any wrong. After all, Ronald, didn't she go to Mass everyday?"

"You're right in saying that she went to Mass everyday. A few Catholics believe that going to Church and praying will save them. In fact, Fr. Murphy told us differently when the Sunday's reading included the Gospel reading of Matthew 25 which, as you might know, is that of the last judgement the separation of the sheep from the goats."

"I remember that vaguely. It made some sense to me far more than what our preacher was saying. Wasn't it about feeding the hungry and clothing the naked?"

"Yes, you're absolutely right. There was no mentioned about blessed are you who prayed and went to church, but rather blessed are those who feed the hungry, and give drink to the thirsty, clothed the naked, looked after the sick and those in prison. "

"I think you missed your calling Ronald. That's the best sermon I'd ever heard. If I heard that years ago even, I might still be going to church."

"What did Fr. Murphy say heaven was like?" asked Mr. Snives.

"I don't think he talked about it that much. He rather gave his ideas on who would be going there, but not about what it would actually be like. He did have a funny notion though which was something to the effect that everyone would be allowed to come in if they wanted to."

"If they wanted to!" said an incredulous Mr. Snives.

"Yeah, I remember that sermon," added Peter. It was strange. Didn't he say that some people wouldn't want to go to heaven? That their pride would keep them from choosing to."

"So, he thinks they chose to burn in hell."

"No," replied Ronald. "Hell is not fire and brimstone according to Fr. Murphy. Hell is not being able to live with God and his love. Hell is living away from God and being in charge of your own life. Much of our modern life is a call to independence, a call to doing your own thing. Just look at our adverts. Treat yourself to this pleasure and that, the best car, and sexy clothes and live surrounded in luxury. Have all this because you deserve it! I really believe that many people will choose the life of luxury and comfort rather than the real life of love. After all we all do that now."

Mr. Snives shook his head: "I don't know what it is but what you say makes a lot of sense. I wonder if I found myself surrounded with comfort again would I think the same way, or perhaps I'm just in a state of shock. Anyway, I'm getting tired. If you two don't mind I'd like to get back to our cave."

"When this is over, I'm going to write a book and call it 'Three Men in a Cave' or 'Modern Cavemen'," laughed Peter.

By the time Mr. Snives made it back to the cave, he was white with shock. Ronald and Peter couldn't remember how to treat shock. They both thought the best thing to do was keep Mr. Snives warm. They luckily had found some matches and started a small fire in the cave with some wood that was already there. Mr. Snives breathing became very irregular.

Mr. Snives looked at Peter and Ronald, "I think I'll be leaving you two now." The two men faded before his eyes. Soon he felt he was hovering above Peter and Ronald and with a bit of shock he saw himself slump before the fire. He looked up and saw a beautiful bright light. He gently floated up to it, at that point, he fell into a deep-peaceful sleep, and he was no longer on earth.

CHAPTER 10

IN-BETWEEN

When Mr. Snives awoke he was lying in a bed still feeling a bit dazed. He looked around and saw several beds like his arranged not in rows like a hospital, but in a regular two-dimensional six-sided-crystal pattern. A soft blue light permeated the room. He watched as others were assisted in their awakening Those helping wore light brown robes and those being helped, like himself, wore a spring green coloured robe. Perhaps he was in a special shelter set up for storm victims.

"Ah, I see you're awake." A man appeared alongside of him. He wore a brown robe and had amazingly bright scintillating eyes. Before he could ask if he was in a hospital the man answered his thought.

"You are not in a hospital Barry. You no longer are on earth, though I think you know that."

"How did you know my name?"

"We are given the names of all the people who awake here."

"Where is here?"

"It's a place in-between. You will slowly be given what you need to know when you are ready. Right now, though, you can join the others." He helped Mr. Snives up and pointed towards an open door. He thanked the man and headed towards the door. He found he had no pain whatsoever. He felt young again!

As he walked on, he saw they were waking up Fr. Murphy and a few other people from Haversay. He saw Veronica Stillwater and started to go to her, but something stopped him. Perhaps he was supposed to go to the door without talking to anyone. He saw one man he thought he recognised but he couldn't remember who he was.

"Where am I?" The big man demanded an answer.

"Please don't shout, Francis. It's not our way here."

"Nobody has called me Francis for years, not since I was a child. Now will you take me to your supervisor so that I can be fully debriefed."

"Actually, Francis, there is no supervisors here. We work as a community and everyone finds out what they must do the same way. If you go out that door you will find others like yourself and from them, you will learn what you have to do."

The big man was very frustrated by now. "You mean I have to ask those ordinary people what's going on. Do you realise who I am?"

"Perhaps the better way to phrase that is who you were. You were Francis Maxwell a multimillionaire who has since passed from the earth and who has no access to his money or its influence." The big man suddenly realised the truth in what the kindly helper said. Without another word, he left the awakening room.

Barry walked behind the big man. They both emerged from the room together. The warm spring air made Barry feel young and alive. He hadn't felt so good in forty years or perhaps ever. They entered a garden that was adjacent to what looked like a very large lake. The lake was so immense he could not see the opposite shore. The still water reflected a golden light. Blooming shrubs were everywhere filling the garden with intoxicating fragrances. Those in charge had placed round wooden tables around the garden and these were almost completely filled with green robed men and women.

"This is beautiful. I wonder if we're in heaven." Mr. Snives was overwhelmed by what he saw. The big man laughed.

"If I'm here it isn't heaven. I don't know where we are and when I asked in there the chap with me said to ask someone else."

Suddenly four bright lights flashed through the sky.

"What the hell was that?" asked Mr. Maxwell.

"Those were souls passing straight to heaven. They've suffered enough and don't need to stop in-between." Mr. Snives was shocked at what he had said. How did he know that? Yet he was certain that what he said was true. Maxwell just grunted and walked on. Something drew them to a table with six others. It appeared that the two seats were the only ones left. The two newcomers joined the other six on the table. They introduced themselves and, as if cued by some hidden director, each revealed his profession on earth. There were five men and three women. The other three men consisted of a carpenter, a burglar, and an advertisement executive. The three women consisted of a science teacher, a prostitute and a doctor. Mr. Snives was the first to ask a question. "Where are we?"

"The woman prostitute was the first to answer." We are in-between what I think is heaven and hell "

"When do we know if we go to heaven or hell?" asked the advertisement executive.

The burglar answered next. "It's not like we've all understood it to be. We actually get to choose whether we go to heaven or hell."

"Choose!" The teacher lifted her head, so her nostrils flared down at the burglar. "That's ridiculous. I've been taught, and I am sure correctly, that we will be judged, and the goats will be separated from the sheep."

"It's not information that he made up," the prostitute added matter-of-factly. "The information that we are sharing has been given to us by whoever is in charge."

"I think someone implanted microchips in our brains. That's why there's no need for computers here." The advertisement executive was happy with what he though was a clever idea.

The carpenter then spoke. "It's not as straight forward as one might think. We have to ask forgiveness for the evil we have done on earth and then and only then will we be allowed to go to heaven."

"Why should that be so difficult?" asked Mr. Maxwell.

"The difficulty is that you will be shown all the harm that you have done and be perfectly sure about this it will be a painful experience. For some the pain will be so terrible that they will choose to go to hell rather than suffer the pain." The carpenter spoke with his normal shy voice yet there was a higher authority in what he said.

"I'm getting some information now," said the doctor. "Do you see that gate over there."

The others looked away from the lake towards the base of a hill where there was a small silver gate, which was across a path leading to a grove of cedars. "It's there that we are to go to confess our offences against humanity. It is there that we will be shown what we have done. We shall be shown what suffering we have caused and perhaps worse what suffering we could have prevented. The name of the garden is Gethsemane!"

The people at the table looked quietly towards the garden. Nobody said anything for quite awhile. A man in a white robe approached the table and began to speak.

"You would be a fool to go into that garden. You know you don't have to. You could stay here as long as you want or you could go to some other place, a place where you don't have to suffer.

"Where are you from?" asked the Banker.

Mr. Maxwell then discovered that he too had some information to share. "You might have said where in the hell are you from because that's where he is from, Hell."

"Some people call it that, but it really isn't all that bad. It's really very much like Earth except better. You'll never die, and your bodies will never grow old. Moreover, in Hell you can be your own man. You can pretty well do what you like."

"What's the bad points then? There must be a reason why hell has such bad press?" asked the advertisement executive.

"That's a good point. Personally, I don't see any. None whatsoever."

"That's because the thought of being near God drives you mad. You hate God and all he represents, "The prostitute looked at the man with disdain."

"I don't deny that. It's just that I can't see why de doesn't allow us to do our own thing. Why do we have to suffer so much to please Him? Why does He demand us to worship him? I just can't see it. And another thing..." Before he could continue the Banker snapped his fingers and the man in the white robe stopped talking.

"How did you do that?" asked Mr. Snives.

"It's easy," responded the Banker. Anyone can snap his or her fingers to stop a temptation here. A double snap will get rid of the chap altogether." To demonstrate his point, he snapped his fingers twice and the man vanished.

"Well, just out of curiosity of course, how can you get him to come back again," asked the teacher.

"Just wish him back."

A soon as he finished speaking a flash of light shot from Gethsemane followed by a man running and screaming out of the garden. Two helpers in brown came running after the man. The man looked at them and screamed. "I won't go back in there. You can't make me." Then three white robe men appeared and surrounded the man. The helpers went away sadly.

The prostitute got up and held her head high. "I think I had better go now or I'll never go. I don't want to sit here thinking how bad it's going to be." She left and walked briskly to the garden gate.

Mr. Maxwell laughed. "I wish I could listen in on her story. I bet it will be X-rated."

The burglar looked contemptuously at Mr. Maxwell: "If there is soon to be a judgement it's not the prostitutes who have the big worries. It's the big wigs like you, the type of people who destroy people's lives with their money. Haven't you heard Mr. Maxwell, 'that's it harder for a rich man to get to heaven then for a camel to pass through a needle's eye.' And one other thing, if you and I are aiming to get to heaven neither one of us will have a job. My talent and yours will not be needed."

The seven people remaining once again became silent. Some were struck by what the young burglar had said: the realisation that all that they strove for in terms of skills, money, position, and even knowledge meant nothing.

"I believe he's right," said the advertisement executive. "It sounds to me that life in heaven might be a bit boring. I mean how is a man to test his mettle. If they're no goals, nothing to achieve what will there be to do? I'm beginning to see why people choose not to go there."

"You mean to tell me that what you were doing on earth really gave you deep down satisfaction. Selling people things that they quite often had no need of?" asked Mr. Snive sincerely.

"Your damn right. I got a buzz out of it. Being able to convince people to do things sometimes they don't even want to do is a fantastic feeling. I never found anything on earth that gave me so much satisfaction."

Mr. Snives shook his head knowingly. "I enjoyed my job when I was younger. It gave me a feeling of importance. My parents were proud to have a son who was a lawyer. People came to me with their legal problems and for advice. But having experienced the destruction my village in one night, made me see how futile all I have done was. I'm glad to be on permanent holiday. I will be pleased to go to a place where there is no need for a lawyer's service."

"I think I'll go for a walk ", said the advertisement executive. He headed towards the lake that was in the opposite direction of the garden. When he was a good distance from the table two men in white robes surrounded him. He seemed to be chatting with them amiably. The next instant he disappeared with the two men. Mr. Snives watched the event with interest.

"I think our advertisement executive made his decision. I wouldn't be surprised if he came back wearing a white robe advertising the advantages of going to Hell. Well friends I think its time for me to go. I also want to get this over with. It reminds me of going to the dentist. You know you need a tooth filled but you also know you don't want the pain. Bye for now."

Mr. Snives stood up. He determinedly headed towards his destination though his legs were unsteady. Just before the entrance of the garden he was overwhelmed by the smell of sensuous perfume that led him to a small secluded area surrounded by shrubs. There he saw a female figure smiling invitingly.

"Perhaps if you rest with me awhile you would feel stronger to face the suffering of the garden. It may be your last chance for some lovely pleasure. I am very capable of engaging both the body and the mind. You'll never experience a mate like me."

"Mr. Snives' young body began to heat with passion. He brought up his hand to snap his fingers. The young agile female gently grabbed his hand before he could respond. Once she held him close, his passion became painfully strong. He closed his eyes and with all his strength snapped his fingers once, then twice. When he opened his eyes, she was gone. He thanked God for the strength to resist and opened the silver gate. He wanted real joy and happiness though he was unsure if he could endure what was needed to win it.

Chapter 11

TRUE HAPPINESS

Barry Snives walked past the gate along a well-marked path. Flowering bushes with large violet and white blossoms lined the path. These gradually faded away and trees took their place shutting out the light of the warm sun. The further he travelled into the garden the dimmer and colder it became. He was beginning to become fearful. It was only his stronger desire for true peace and happiness that drove him forward. He wasn't a Christian and in his adult life God had lost all significance. He only relied on himself and his talents and effort. He was polite and friendly to all he met and even kind. He would never again give his heart to another human being: to love was too painful for him.

The path, by now quite narrow, led him to an opening of short green grass in which stood eight old gnarled olive trees. The trees looked centuries old. A worn patch of ground in the centre of the trees drew him. By now the light was so dim it was as if it was night. The cold pierced his bones and his body ached to be in the warm sun, which he had so recently left. Yet, he persevered. He knelt down on the worn patch of grass and waited.

He began to think of his past life and at first, his thoughts were dim perceptions with only vague details. The vague thoughts then became vivid and a guiding light transported him to the past.

He now was a spectator as he watched his life unfold with its sorrows and joys. Like all humans, relationships formed Barry's life. He lived in a small house with his mother, father and younger sister. His father was a gardener and his mother was a secretary. When he was younger, he enjoyed his family and the love they gave him. His father and mother dearly loved both of their children, their son, who was obviously clever, and the daughter who wasn't. When he was about ten years old, he began to compare his family with others. He, by then, was well aware of his intelligence and he was painfully aware that his sister was retarded. Up to that point, he was always his sister's protector and playmate.

One of the lovely things he did with his sister was to take her to the films every Saturday. She really enjoyed that. His parents gladly gave him the money to take her there. One day a school friend remarked on this: "It must be boring taking your thick sister to the movies every Saturday."

"My sister is not thick!" responded Barry defensively but at that moment, he became ashamed of being with her and he never took her to a film again.

He also used to read her a story in the evening. Barry loved reading and loved literature. He enjoyed it as much as his sister did. Sadly, because of his painful awareness of his sister's lack of intelligence, he stopped that. The invisible guide made Barry see the pain he caused his sister as he re-lived one horrible night. It was the second night that he refused to read to his sister. She came to the bedroom to ask for a story.

"Barry, why have you stopped reading me stories. I love them so much." She began to softly cry.

"Go away cry baby. I have more important things to do like my homework." Barry saw his sister go away in tearful rejection.

"Oh God, why did I do that. Please, please forgive me. I didn't want to hurt her."

It was shortly after that day that his sister went into a deep depression and never recovered. Tears came in streams down Barry's face. He wished he could have turned the clock back to be able once again to hug his sister and to tell her that he loved her.

His life continued to unfold. He saw himself when he first went to university, the first one of his family to do so. He wanted to be a success not only for himself but also for his parents' sake. He studied hard and had little time or money for a social life. At first, he was quite content with this way of life but gradually envy crept into his conscience and he wanted what many of the other students had, money, cars and nice-looking clothes. He wanted not only to be a successful student but to have a career that would make him financially successful. It was then that he decided to become solicitor rather than his first love, a writer. He also knew that in order to be successful he had to know the right people. . His own family had no useful connections, so he had to find the right friends.

When his grandfather died, he was left with a tidy sum with which he could launch his new social life. He carefully cultivated the right friends and soon they invited him into their homes. Of course, this brought up the difficult problem of return invitations. How could he invite his highly educated rich friends to his parents' humble cottage with a father who was a gardener and mother who was a secretary? Therefore, he told his friends that his mother was dying of cancer, so no one asked to come see him.

His parents attempted several times to see him at the university where he was a boarder, but he always managed to put them off.

"Son why is it that you don't want us to come to see you at your university. Every time we want to go you always have something to do."

"I have to work all the time Dad. There just isn't any time while I'm studying."

Finally, his father, who was no fool, bluntly said: "You are ashamed of us. Now that you are educated and have sophisticated friends, you want nothing to do with us. You might as well throw us away as so much rubbish!"

"No, father, that is not true. I love you and Mother."

Though Barry denied it, he knew what his father said was true. He lusted after success to such an extent that he lost his ability to love. When he lived in Haversay, everyone thought highly of him though no one was close to him.

"Oh God, I can hardly take the pain you have shown me. Please forgive me." Deep with in his soul was etched the hurt expressions of his mother and father. He knew now that he would experience even more pain. He heard a sharp voice telling him to run away while he could.

"God only wants you to suffer," it said.

"No", he nearly shouted. "I need to know the truth! I want to be free" In response, the day of his wedding came into focus. His wife came from a working-class family like himself and so there were need to hide the fact that he did also. He really did love his bride to be. He felt for the first time in his life full of joy. He was ready to give himself to her and cherish her for better or for worse. Of course, as is normal, much of his love was passion. Nevertheless, his love was sincere.

The first few months of the marriage were fine. His wife became pregnant and bore him a lovely daughter. Then, as the novelty of being married became routine, he once again turned towards his first love, success.

His wife used to greet him every time he came home. She listened to his difficulties at work and how hard he had to work. He asked less and less about how she and his daughter, Jenni were. Allison decided that he no longer cared about them. She became sad a lonely and then, at the insistence of a friend, took up teaching young children in a voluntary nursery. She found meaning for her life there and new friendships. Sadly, though, she and Barry continued to drift apart. She no longer met him at the door when he came home. He hardly noticed.

He knew something was missing in his life. He had success working for a small well-established law firm yet happiness eluded him. The crisis came in the third year of his marriage. His wife had been going out at night 'with friends'. He never thought much of what she was doing because he never asked or was interested. He assumed they were girl friends.

One evening he was driving home much later than usual. He and his partners had a difficult meeting over a potential lawsuit. A client alleged that the legal costs charged by the firm for the processing of his father's estate were unnecessarily high and he was seeking a substantial rebate. Unfortunately, Barry was responsible for this client and it looked as if the other partners might ask him to go because of it.

As he was driving home, he decided to stop at a pub not far from his home. He drove into the car park and was about to go in when he saw a couple getting into a car. The light was not good, so the couple's features were not clear. When the man opened the door for the woman, he gently kissed her. As she got in the car, the light reflected off her face; it was the face of his wife!

He decided to have a few drinks before he confronted her with the evidence. How could she be so unfaithful? I have never looked at a woman before, he thought. I would never do such a thing. Now as he looked at his past from the cold calmness of the garden, he could painfully see that he had been blatantly unfaithful. He had ignored his wife and treated her and his daughter as property. He watched himself coming home from the pub.

He opened the door only to find that his wife was not there . The baby-sitter had long since put his daughter to bed.

"Hello, Mr. Snives. I was hoping you would come home soon. I was getting a bit sleepy. I'll call Dad and he'll come and pick me up."

"Did Mrs Snives say she would be late?"

"Oh, she's left a letter for you. She's not coming home tonight." Mr. Snives held his emotions until her father picked up the girl. He didn't dare read the letter while the sitter was there. He poured himself a strong whiskey and sat down to read it.

Dear Barry,
I suppose you will be surprised to get this letter. Basically, all I want from you
is a divorce. You have really left me already. I have found some else and he
and I are in love. I don't want a penny from you. I just want to be free of the
pretence of our marriage. I want to be free of your cold indifference and
uncaring ways.

I do love Jenni and she loves me as well as you. I will be back tomorrow and we can then decide what is best for her.

Allison.

What had happened that night completely devastated Barry. How could he have been so blind? He was angered with his wife and her obvious infidelity. He was disappointed that she wasn't going to fight for some of his hard-earned money. He would love to see her try. However, he was relieved because he dearly loved his money and possessions. He decided he would fight for the child's custody, but from the letter it appeared that she might not even oppose him in this, but did he really want to care for a little girl by himself?

He was then shown the day he and his wife and child parted. It was a cold wet morning. Allison had come to ask him to sign some papers so that she could get a divorce as quickly as possible. That day bitterness and hatred filled him so when she came to the door with his daughter Jenni, he was ready to express that hatred.

"Ah the whore has come for legalisation of her state."

Allison was not prepared for Barry's venomous attack.

"Are you mad. What are you going to gain by using such foul language in front of our child? What's wrong with you?"

"Wrong, wrong. You don't know. You are unfaithful and bent on tearing our family apart and you ask me what is wrong?"

"Barry please, just sign the paper and I'll take my offensive self our of your sight."

He grabbed the paper and signed it. He tossed the paper contemptuously at her.

"Well it's goodbye to bad rubbish," he continued. She took the paper and the child who was now in tears to the door. As she left, he slammed the door and with the slam of the door, his life had changed forever: love of any form would play no part in his life. He was essentially dead.

"Oh God, I didn't want her to leave or the child. I said what I said because I was hurt."

A gradually gentle warming replaced the coldness of the garden. A warm light began to engulf him, and he knew that God had forgiven him. He then saw as in a vision his wife and child. Allison was smiling warmly, and his little girl was waving. Tears of joy gushed from his eyes. He sobbed uncontrollably. When he had finished the warm presence that he felt before once again covered him like a mantle. He had found his peace.

He felt himself directed up another path away from the others. There he saw others like himself, dressed in green and all waiting in silence. He joined the silent group and waited with them.

Chapter 12

MIGUEL and PEDRO

Pedro and Miguel awoke together. They stepped through the door into the beautiful garden.

"How is it that we made it to Heaven, Pedro?" asked Miguel.

"You fool. This can't be Heaven. We are murderers and drug smugglers. Do you think we could ever get to heaven?"

"My mother always taught me that God loves us no matter what we did."

"You've got it wrong my friend. Haven't you heard of Hell, the place where all sinners go? There you'll burn for all eternity"

Two men in white coats approached them before they could reach their table. They had dark olive skin and spoke in Spanish.

"Welcome Pedro, welcome Miguel. I am Pepe and this is Juan. I couldn't help over hearing what you said about Hell. Pedro, there is no place where you burn forever. I am not saying that a place called Hell doesn't exist. It's just not like you have been told."

Miguel looked suspiciously at the two smiling men. They reminded him of similar men on Earth, men who would sell their families into slavery if they would profit from it.

Pedro's response was different. He saw in these men kindred hearts. Men who love to manipulate other men. Men who liked to use weaker men.

"So, tell us about your place, Hell. Why do you like it so much?" Pedro asked.

"Because you can live for ever and you can be your own man. You can do what you want to do"

"You make it sound so good. Why aren't you enjoying it now? Why are you doing this recruiting bit," replied Pedro who understood his own kind.

"We understand each other, Pedro. Of course, we have incentives for each man we bring along. However, we have little influence on a person's choice. Each man has to make up his own mind. We are here to expedite the arrival of the best candidates."

"Why is Hell so much better than heaven? Why shouldn't we want to go to heaven?" asked a suspicious Miguel. Juan spoke to Miguel kindly and softly as if he was one of his many uncles:

"Miguel, I must make you aware of some very hard facts. It is true the occasional murderer and drug runner makes it to heaven. I must warm you it will be painful. You both have committed some terrible crimes. You particularly would find it difficult to reach heaven Pedro. Not only did you kill several men, but also you enjoyed every minute of it. Killing to you was a form of entertainment. You would have to spend an eternity asking forgiveness from Him. Begging Him for the chance to be with Him and never being able to do what you like, but only what He wants. We can't see any reason for wanting to go to Heaven if that's the case. There are only real men in Hell, men who know what they want. And the women are quite real too."

Miguel countered, "I believe my mother when she said God loves us. I know it's true."

"We are not allowed to lie and therefore I would have to agree with you. Remember though, he has to love everyone there, including the people that you have killed. Do you think they would want you there with them? They and you would agree that it would be unfair you were allowed in Heaven after killing them"

"Go away, I think you are distorting the truth" With that, the men vanished from sight. Pedro was quite angry by Miguel's actions.

"Why did you do that? I wanted to talk with them further."

"I am sure you will have the chance. For me, I have spent enough time on earth talking with such men. I know what they are like and they would sooner slit your throat than want to help you." The two men walked to their table in silence.

Pedro was a son of a plumber who had his own business. He was the second oldest in his family which consisted of an older sister a year older than he and a brother three years younger. He was a quite placid boy until he became a teenager. Then he gradually became more vicious. He was bigger and stronger than boys his age and he loved to bully them. One day he was fighting a boy and had him on the ground.

"Say give, you little moron." he taunted. The young boy refused, and Pedro then pinned both his arms to the ground with his legs and began pounding the boy in the face until it was a mass of red blood. He might have killed him if a man hadn't come along and pulled him off.

Pedro's parents were shocked when they discovered what he had done. They told him off fiercely hoping that would be enough to deter him from doing the same thing again, but there was something sinister about their son that frightened both parents. Pedro on his part was not repentant at all. All his peers now feared him and that pleased him. He knew he would do what he did again, and he knew he would enjoy it. To his selfish mind, people were there to give him pleasure. Their only intrinsic value was to serve him. He saw people as things he could use.

His father wanted him to join him in the family business, but he had no desire to get his hands dirty. When he was in his twenties, he hardly worked at all. He would be missing from home for weeks at a time and when he was there, he intimidated his parents. In the end, they threw him out after he had assaulted his father.

His desire to see others suffer up to that point only amounted to him beating them near to death. He made sure no one saw him when he attacked other men and though he was larger and stronger than most men, he rarely picked a fight with someone as big as he was.

Pedro carried a large switchblade with him in case his physical strength let him down. A brother of a teenage boy he had severely beaten confronted him one evening. The man, called Mateo, was as large as Pedro and an excellent fighter. Pedro knew the odds were against him, but he was prepared. It was late in the evening as they faced each other in a deserted alley in Madrid.

"You, scum. You've nearly killed my brother. He is only 16, just a boy."

"And I'll do the same to you, you ***** head."

"We shall see about that." They faced each other. The man waited for Pedro to move and when he wouldn't he struck him in the face knocking him down. The blow came so quickly that Pedro couldn't stop it. He knew this man was far better fighter than he, and that he might soon be killed. He grabbed his knife as he got up and faced the man threateningly.

"So the scum needs a knife to face me. He's not enough of a man without it."

"I'm not a fool. But I think you are and soon to be a dead one." The man unsuccessfully lunged for the knife. Pedro stepped aside and then jabbed the knife into his stomach. He twisted the knife and once again he felt an enjoyment as he watched the man die.

"I will see you in Hell," he screamed as he died.

Pedro knew that even the dumbest detective would connect him to the killing. It would be only a matter of time before they caught him. He needed to get out of the country and quick. He contacted Dan Radcliff who recruited him and smuggled him out of the country. Radcliff knew that Pedro would give him no trouble. If he did, he would turn him over to the police. The man he killed came from a rich and powerful family who would make sure he got what he deserved.

Pedro and Miguel found their table, which had three seats empty. The five people at the table stopped talking when they approached. A tall distinguished looking gentleman with thick grey hair stood to greet them. He held out his strong well-shaped hand to Pedro. "My name is Daniel, I was a teacher in life," he said proudly.

Pedro smiled maliciously, "I was a murderer and a drug smuggler. I have never killed a teacher though," he added.

"I see," he said. "And you are not repentant of what you did, even here?" The man released Pedro hands thoughtfully.

"No, I am not. Why should I be?"

Miguel reached out his hand to the man:

"My name is Miguel. I am sorry to say that I too have killed as well as smuggled drugs. Unlike Pedro, I am ashamed of what I did. I started my life of crime out of necessity, not out of boredom. I was trapped in a life of crime."

A young frail looking woman greeted Miguel:

"I was called Sister Agnes when I was on earth. I worked with Mother Teresa's helpers in New York. Many people use drugs there, especially the young. I know what drugs do to people. I also know that God will forgive all who ask him. So, trust in Him Miguel."

"Thank you, Sister."

Sister then turned to Pedro:

"Pedro, do you know that drugs can destroy a life slowly and painfully like a cancer. How can you say you are not sorry for what you did?"

"It's simple. I don't care for other people. Living in New York you certainly notice that how everyone lives for themselves. Every man is selfish, some just pretend they're not. Even you so called do-gooders. You just get a kick out of helping people like I do seeing them suffer."

"I would never have understood that people choose to go to Hell when I was on Earth. But talking with you makes me see that. You don't want to know God's love. You want to be your own man. I'm sorry for you." The sister looked at him with sad and compassionate eyes and shook her head.

Before Pedro could reply, another man spoke.

"This conversation is very interesting, Pedro. I'm not surprised at what a twisted mind you have. I've seen you work."

Pedro focused on the man who was speaking.

"Ah, it is the unfortunate Inspector Maxwell. You never did get us for anything. It was funny how Mr. Radcliff gave himself up. If he didn't you would be still trying to catch him." Inspector Maxwell looked hatefully at Pedro. What he said was too true.

Maxwell continued speaking wanting to know the truth. Were the drugs coming the night he died in the restaurant or was he wasting his time. Did Radcliff have the last victory?

"Just an academic point now Pedro, but I would like to know if the drugs where coming to El Faro the night we all died."

"I think you will never give up being an inspector, and in that case, you may be down with me. The drugs were never meant to come there. You wasted your time and energy for nothing. Mr. Radcliff was always smarter than you. How does it feel to be a loser?" Inspector Maxwell sat silently thinking of his wasted life and wondering why he had never had the success others did.

"Murderer," shouted a man nearly running towards the table. "I said I would see you in hell."

Pedro got up and prepared to face the angered Mateo whom he had killed.

"No, Mateo. Do not harm Pedro."

"Harm me. I killed him once and I can do it again."

"No, you can not Pedro. No harm can come to anyone here." As if to prove her wrong Pedro went to slap the nun. When he struck her, he screamed in pain. He felt as if he struck solid stone! Mateo stopped in front of his murderer knowing he too would only hurt himself if he struck Pedro.

The nun turning to Mateo said, "You see Mateo here you can learn the truth. If you continue to hate Pedro, you will only end up hating yourself."

"Come with me Mateo," shouted Pedro, "I'm sure we can find a place where I can slowly kill you again."

Mateo looked at the pathetic Pedro and then the little nun.

"Thank you, sister. I will let him go to Hell by himself."

Pedro snarled like the animal that he was.

"Do gooders, cops and cowards can go to a place where they are told what to do. Real men go where I'm going." With that, he walked away and immediately two escorts dressed in white joined him. A thick grey misted covered the three and then evaporated into nothing. Pedro had made his choice.

Miguel watched all of this with interest. He looked at the sister sitting at the table.

"Sister, I am truly sorry for what I have done. Will He forgive me?"

"If you are truly sorry, you will be forgiven. Before you are forgiven you must go to Gethsemane to see the consequences of your sins. It will not be easy," she warned.

Miguel got up and started walking towards the Garden.

An ugly man dressed in white snarled at Miguel, "Where do you think your going, Heaven? No way man, you're..." Miguel snapped his fingers and the man vanished. As he walked into the Gethsemane, he started to shiver. It was dark and cold when he arrived at the centre where the olive trees were. There he knelt down and began to pray for forgiveness. A repulsive rodent like creature the size of a large dog appeared from behind the closest olive tree.

"You will have to pay for what you did. You'll see all the pain you caused and then you will experience the worst pain of your life"

A man illuminated by a bright light appeared and commanded the creature to depart:

"Be gone father of all lies. You speak a truth but yet it is twisted." The creature covered its eyes and fled from the man. The man spoke with a deep commanding voce:

"There is some truth in what he has said. You will suffer but it is only so that your healing can be complete. Like the operations on earth, it will be painful. The pain will be one of recognition and sorrow and from it, by the grace of our God, you will be healed."

Miguel felt at peace for the first time since he was a boy of sixteen. The time just before his father had died. He lived in Cartagena with his father, mother and two younger brothers and a younger sister. His father was a headwaiter in a hotel there. He made enough money for his family to live comfortably in a bungalow in a nearby village. Those were happy days for Miguel. He had no worries and no responsibilities other than working part time in a local grocery shop and doing his homework.

All that change when his father died suddenly of a heart attack. He had not taken out an insurance policy and the family had no other means of support. The larger family gave a meagre support, but that was all they could do. Miguel's family was very poor.

Miguel found himself as the head of the house and the main breadwinner. Though he was proud to do this, the responsibility frightened him. He had to quit school, which he found difficult since it meant forgoing the social life and the sports, which he loved. He was a good footballer and hoped to take it up professionally. All those hopes collapsed before him. He now had to support a large family.

He went to Cartagena looking for a full-time job. He found a job as a waiter but quickly discovered that the money he received a week only covered a few days' costs of housing and food needed for the family. He was desperate. The rent was in arrears by three months and his family, and particular his mother, was fearful that the owner would soon evict them from their home, the only home Miguel ever knew. It was then that he looked for any means of keeping the family afloat. He was street wise enough to know how to get into contact with people who dealt with drugs. He started moving marijuana by truck from southern Spain to the *la fueras* of Madrid where it was either smuggled into the city or it abroad. He lasted at that job for several years before the police caught him. His mother was devastated when she discovered that he had smuggled drugs and was going to prison. The owner, an English man , eventually evicted his family from their home. Soon after the eviction, the house mysteriously burnt down. What Miguel tried to prevent had occurred anyway.

"Was it painful to watch your house burn, Miguel?" asked the angel.

"Yes, and especially to know that it was my fault."

"Well, Miguel, let me show you all the homes that you helped to destroy with the drugs you smuggled." He forced Miguel to watch the procession of broken lives of those who used the smuggled drugs.

"Please, stop!" cried Miguel. "I cannot take anymore."

"If you stop now you will never be healed, and only those who are healed will enter fully into the Master's kingdom."

"Continue then, I want to be healed." After the torment of seeing the pain and suffering he had caused, he sweated blood. He was a man truly in anguish.

His pain was not over yet. He had to see his life after he had left Spain and joined with Dan Radcliff. During this part of his life, he not only aided the drug runners, but he had actually killed a man. He hated all Englishmen because the man who had evicted his family was English. It was an English police detective that he killed and neatly disposed of the body. No one ever knew, except perhaps Dan Radcliff, that he was the murderer.

"There is one more thing I need to show you. I must show you some of the pain who caused to the policeman's family when you killed him."

Miguel never thought about the man's family. He was just fearful that they would catch him. He should have realised that in the end all men must pay for the wrongs they did while on earth. He now was made to see the grief he had caused a wife and mother of three young children when they received the news of her husband's death.

Miguel saw the family in their house just before the news of the policeman's death. The three children were playing in the garden while the mother was knitting and watching.

"Mommy, are we going to have another brother? Her little son of four looked up at his mother.

Then the older pushed in alongside him. " I want a sister. Boys are only trouble and besides there are two boys in the family already. Tell him mommy that we're going to have a baby sister"

The mother laughed. "I don't really know darling. But no matter what Daddy and I will love it just as much as we love you." Just then the front bell rang.

"It must be Daddy," said the smallest. "He'll know if it will be a boy or a girl."

"I do not want to watch this," cried Miguel. I am sorry for what I have done, but please don't make me watch this." There was no reply from the angel. Miguel bowed his head and let the scene unfold.

The little boy ran to the door.

"Mommy it's Daddy's partner, Dick."

"Oh my God, screamed the mother." Miguel's knife had destroyed a happy family.

Miguel turned as cold as ice.

"I don't want to accept that I did this." The angel put his hand on Miguel's shoulder. Just ask His forgiveness Miguel. Miguel stood frozen with the forces of good and evil battling for his soul.

Chapter 13

THE RULE BOOK

Inspector Henry Maxwell sat staring in the direction of Gethsemane. A brilliant light flashed from its centre reminding him that Miguel was there. Surely, this means that the murderer has gone to Hell he thought to himself. Perhaps with all those murderers, thieves and drug dealers in Hell there is a need for a man with my talent. All his life he made sure he followed the rules and regulations set down for him. He never thought about the system being right or wrong. He found it easier just to follow it. He made sure he ordered his life and he disdained those lives that were not. He was a perfectionist and proud of it. To give him credit he did work hard, but when his hard work achieved no results, he felt cheated.

He was shocked to see Dan Radcliff heading towards his table. The man who had humiliated him and had caused him to lose his life was swiftly approaching. Dan introduced himself to those who were at the table. He turned to Maxwell and offered his hand.

"Inspector Maxwell, you have caught me at last." The Inspector gave Radcliff a hard stare causing Radcliff to withdraw his hand.

"No, Radcliff, I haven't caught you, but I'll be here to watch you go to Hell."

"I don't want to go to Hell my friend. I wasn't a good man to say the least, but I am genuinely sorry for what I have done."

"I suppose you simply think you can say sorry and that will be it," sneered the Inspector?

"No, that wouldn't be fair. I'm willing to pay for what I've done. I trust God will do what is right."

"You're a fool. If a man like you went to Heaven, then there would be no justice. If you are accepted there then I would rather go to Hell."

"Don't say such a thing, Inspector," pleaded Sr. Agnes. "God wants to forgive us all. He really doesn't want to send anyone to Hell."

"Are you saying he doesn't deserve to go to Hell?"

"No, I would rather say none of us deserve Heaven, but that's what God wants for us.

Don't you remember the story of the Prodigal Son? How the father constantly waited hoping his son would come back even though he left the family taking his share of the inheritance with him. The father was overjoyed to see the son. He never had any thoughts of condemning him. It's only men that enjoy condemning other men."

"I do remember that awful story. I don't understand why he let the younger son get away with it. He should have punished the younger son. The older brother was right. What good does it do to be faithful if those who aren't receive the same reward? There's no justice in that."

A woman o came running out from the Gethsemane Garden screaming in anger and interrupted the dialogue:

"It's not fair, it's not fair. I went to Church everyday. I prayed everyday. I helped with every activity possible at the church. I'm told I didn't do enough. I'm told to repent for putting myself above my neighbours who didn't go to church. He told me that I gossiped, and that gossip harmed many people. It's not fair! The priest never said I was doing wrong. He never condemned me. He never told me to stop gossiping. I will be damned if He expects me to forgive my abusing, drunken husband. It's he that deserves Hell."

The woman's outcry brought an instant response. Two brown robed helpers flanked her on one side and two men dressed in white were on the other side. She looked at one and then the other. One of the men dressed in white then spoke.

"She has clearly made her decision to come with us. You said you didn't want to forgive your husband, didn't you?" The lady nodded uncertainly. "Then you can't go to Heaven because they insist on you forgiving everyone. Ask them if you think I'm not telling the truth."

She looked at the brown robed men. "Can't I go without forgiving him?"

The two men had to tell her the hard truth:

"They are correct. Forgiving your husband is only for your healing. God is not asking you to do that for His pleasure in seeing you suffer. He knows that he can only fill you with his love if you forgive all that have hurt you. It's for your own good."

"I'm sorry then. He asked too much." She turned towards the men dressed in white and they left together.

"Perhaps what people have called heaven isn't what we thought it was. It sounds like a getaway for criminals and the outcasts of society. The people who hate the law," Maxwell said bitterly.

"There will be only one law in Heaven and that's the law of Love," replied Sister Agnes.

Inspector Maxwell pondered the possibilities to himself. Perhaps my father will be in Heaven doing nothing but reading poetry. Something's terribly wrong. What happen to the idea of right and wrong? They should uphold the law-abiding citizens and reward them. It appears that Heaven is just the opposite. Those who followed the rules lose and those who don't are forgiven. What kind of justice is that?"

He entered the Garden of Gethsemane not as a repentant sinner but a man who was demanding answers. He marched to the centre of the Garden where the olive trees stood and waited. All that greeted him was an uncertain silence. He had to do more to get a response, but he wasn't sure what to do, or was it that he knew what he had to do but didn't want to.

In frustration he shouted, "Are you a God who laughs at us who obey the law or not?" The answer was swift and certain; a brilliant but painful light surrounded him, and the earth shook under his feet so violently that it threw him to the ground. When he awoke, he was back in time, watching his father smoking his pipe and sitting at his desk.

His father was a poet of little renown who had published enough poems so that one might consider him a poet though not near enough to make a living for his wife and two children. The Inspector's mother had to work full time as a secretary to pay for the rent and food the family needed every week. Even with her working a job and a half, the family barely survived.

When he was younger, he enjoyed his father's creative side but as he became older, he began to see his father in the eyes of his disillusioned mother, as a drunk and dreamer.

One night his father never came home. He discovered that the police arrested him for disorderly conduct, and he spent the night in jail. The fine he received was more than he had received for his last published poem. His father came home condemning the stupid ignorant police who had put him in jail.

"Henry, if you ever become a policeman, I'll never speak to you again," he said while recovering from his hangover. It was then he decided to become a policeman. He decided to take the job most hated by his father the poet because he saw his father as ineffective and useless. He wanted to be different. He wanted to build his life on certainty, not based on things such as poetry and love. He saw rules and the law as something certain. When people like his father broke the law, judges rightly fined them or put them in jail. By being a policeman, he would bring certainty into his life.

His brother David was more like his father. He was carefree and had the heart of a poet. He loved the company of other people whether discussing literature or just having a good time. At sixteen David was already drinking but in moderation. Some of his friends smoked marijuana, but David drew the line there refusing it when offered. His father's bout with alcohol convinced him that it could cause trouble.

David had a friend who was dying of cancer. He was under going chemotherapy and was suffering terribly with nausea and vomiting. David heard that a small dose of marijuana would help so he used to buy a little for him when he went to visit. The young man was pleased with the gift since the marijuana did lessen his feeling of nausea. His brother Henry found one of the packets in David's room. He decided to teach his brother a lesson to stop him from breaking the law, so he called the police and reported him.

The police came and arrested David. His father and mother were in shock with their son being charged with possession of the drug and the fact that his own brother turned him in.

"Henry, how could you turn in your brother? What has he done to you?" asked his mother.

"He was breaking the law. I just wanted to frighten him so that he would stop. I'm sure they won't do much to him."

Henry's father was furious. He disliked his condescending son before this incident and now he hated him:

"That bastard would turn us in if we were breaking his precious law. He's a monster without a heart!"

Henry with hardly an expression replied, "Yes, you're right. I would." His mother who was usually timid and who hated arguments needed more.

"Why, though. Why are you so concerned with the law? Why should it matter to you more than your own flesh and blood? Doesn't your brother mean anything to you?"

Henry thought for a moment and then responded in an even tone, "I guess not."

His mother sat down and began to cry uncontrollably.

"What have we done wrong?"

Unmoved Henry watched the scene from the past. Brilliant and painful light engulfed him. A voice thundered from the source of the light.

"How could you cause such pain and still not care?"

Even before this heavenly accuser Henry was unrepentant.

"I was doing what was right. The law was on my side. David had broken the law."

"But he spent two years in prison. Your mother died soon afterwards, and you still feel no remorse. Don't you realise that because you are afraid to love you hide behind the law. It's there that you feel safe."

"My father was a great one for love. He only brought grief."

"He was weak, Henry, like all humans. You must forgive him and then you will be free to love. You will then find peace."

"Is he, my father, in heaven?"

"Yes."

"Then I'm not sure if I want to be there with him."

Inspector Maxwell left the garden not knowing what to do. He knew he would be welcomed back if he came with a repentant heart. He walked alone along the shore of the still lake. He looked to the distant shore and noticed a grey mist forming on the horizon. Up to this time there was only the warm sun shining from a clear blue sky. A man dressed in white suddenly appeared in front of him startling him.

"People think they have forever to make their eternal decision, but time is now short."

Before Maxwell could ask what he meant, the man continued:

"You may wonder what a person like you can do in Hell. I can truthfully say you could help enforce our laws. You see, Hell is a place where laws are the only things that make people work together. Of course, there are the constant warring kingdoms otherwise how would we keep our generals happy. Within a kingdom, there are laws you could enforce. You could be part of a law enforcement team which locks up criminals and once there usually tortures and executes them."

"Executes! Does that mean they no longer will exist?"

"No, they would be brought back to life. That's what makes Hell so interesting. People can keep on dying. I think I'm revealing too much. What I'm saying my friend is that Hell is a place where you can lock up the poets who break the law."

The man vanished before Maxwell could reply. He still was undecided as to what to do.

A cold breeze drifted across the lake and Maxwell felt the chill. The dark grey mist was growing.

Many of the tables were now empty or half empty. There was one full table left, and no one seemed to want to move from it. The spirit of indecision was certainly in full presence there. Only two at the table were not from Haversay, an advertising agent Phil Earl and an arms dealer David Foulgate. Those from Haversay were Father Michael Murphy, Bishop John Devon, Margarita and Charles from El Faro and the village's gossips Veronica Stillwater and Penelope Barnes. They felt the cold from the growing mist across the lake.

"I cannot understand why you and Father Murphy are just waiting here. Surely you of all people should know what to do." Veronica Stillwater really was sincere in what she said.

Charles answered with a laugh.

"You are a foolish woman. These priests know nothing. They pretend to know, but in truth they are as ignorant as the rest of us as to what really happens after death. They cling to their rules and regulations and endlessly try to make us feel like dirt. I was a Catholic once. I was baptised and confirmed. I really believed all the crap they claimed to know. Then a drunken driver killed my sister. He took her life and the bastard didn't even care. They gave him two years in prison, but he was soon out. The priest who buried her told me that unfortunately all men must die because of their sins and it was just time for God to take her."

"I always thought God was a loving God. How could he have allowed my sister to die with so much pain and her so young? She was only eight when she was murdered. Do these priests really know why young innocent people have to die? Hey, Bishop can you give me an answer?" He sneered at both men daring them to attempt an answer.

"You're right in many way, Charles. We don't know what we are talking about. People like to be told an absolute answer. They feel insecure if they don't receive one. How could I, as a bishop, say I didn't know?"

"But surely what we teach and say is based on the Church's teaching. Of course, it must be true or least in most parts." Father Murphy could not accept the Bishop's answer.

"I never was a Christian," interjected David Foulgate, "but I read Medieval History at Cambridge and I am well versed on indulgences and the inquisition. In both cases, the Catholic Church was totally wrong. The most stupid thing I had ever read was an account of the Dominican Inquisitors burning a Jewish heretic and then having the temerity to offering indulgences to those who came to watch!"

"I have no idea if the incident was true or not. It just shows people's weakness and lust for power. On Earth I would have said it was Catholic doctrine, but here what difference does it make."

The Bishop spoke as if his real thoughts were elsewhere. He was thinking about his imminent judgement and about the awesome responsibility he had had on Earth. He knew he had much to answer for. Too often he had answered others with the party line, not daring to say what he really knew was true. He valued his position too much. He liked being called Bishop.

"Bishop, I was forced into prostitution. Will I be kept from heaven because of it?"

"I don't know who is going to heaven or is going to Hell. I don't even know where I'm going!"

"Ah ha, now I hear a priest speaking the truth," gloated Charles. Father Murphy was getting fed up with Charles who he had no liking for even on Earth.

"If you want to know the truth then why don't you go to the Garden? I'm sure God will tell you the truth. And I wouldn't be surprised if some of the truth about you is that you have used the excuse of your sister's death to lead the selfish life that you did."

"I don't see you going there, priest. In fact, I don't see anyone here making a decision. Who's going to be the first to decide to go to Heaven or Hell?"

Charles' challenged was ignored. An emaciated creature stumbling along the lake's shore distracted the group. The man faced the growing mist and shook his fists at it as if to challenge it to devour him. He turned towards the group and smiled grimly.

"I know that man," said Margarita.

CHAPTER 14

THE GOSSIPS

Fr. Murphy squinted his eyes to get a better look at the man who was only fifty metres away.

"The man looks like a demon."

"He is," said Margarita. "He's the reason why we are here. He's the man who could have saved our lives but didn't because he didn't want to look the fool. He is Paul Thorne the head of the Met office."

All at the table had reason to hate this man. He was responsible for not warning them to evacuate. He looked again at those sitting at the table and responded with a hideous grin. He then began to shout at the people including those at the full table:

"I'm warning you a storm is coming far worse than you had in England. This one will last for all eternity."

"Fate has many twists," the Bishop commented as if he was watching a play and not his own destiny unfolding. "This man may be working out his redemption by warning us now of a different type of storm. One that will make our eternal decision for us if we don't make one soon."

"What do you mean Bishop? Surely, God will decide where we will go. What does this storm have to do with it?" Penelope was truly perplexed by the prophecy.

"What the Bishop is saying my dear lady is that this island or what ever it is will soon be no more. We all will have to make a decision, or I believe we will be on our way to Hell. I'm sure that's where I'm going anyway. I would really like to be with my friends."

"How do you know your friends will be in Hell."

"I don't think you'll find many arms dealers in Heaven," replied David Foulgate. "After all, the product we sold killed people and nothing else. And the money countries spend on arms is a good chunk of their budgets, especially the poorer countries. Can you imagine the lives my company and I destroyed? The thing is I'm not repentant.   I never broke the law once. I made a good living from what I did and I brought a lot of revenue into the country. My company and I also provided many jobs for the area where my factory was. But I don't think God will see it that way."

"I think you are correct," said Fr. Murphy.

Veronica abruptly stood up:

"Let's go into the Garden, now Penelope. I think what they are saying is that if we don't, we'll be stuck here or pushed into Hell by the storm. We really should be all right. After all, we've never killed anyone or stole money from anyone. We went to church regularly and even did the flowers. If murderers and drug dealers have a chance, certainly we do. Are you coming dear?" With her little speech Veronica and Penelope said goodbye to the group and left with confidence for what they hoped would be a slight telling off for their little and harmless sins.

Fr. Murphy watched them go before he spoke:

"If I understand my theology at all I think they are going to have a harder time than they think. After all, I did explain to both of them what Christ was saying in Matthew 25, when he separated the sheep and goats. Those who will enter His kingdom may or may not have gone to church. They were all accepted for what they did to the least of there fellow man."

"I agree Michael," said the Bishop. "I think they are in for bit of a shock."

The women quickly entered the garden.

"Oh, Veronica it's awful dark and cold here. I really wish we could have a cup of tea to warm and comfort us"

"I totally agree with you. I suppose we'll have to wait. I'm sure once we get to Heaven there will be an ample supply of the best tea we ever drank."

"Sorry, ladies. There will be no tea in Heaven." The man in white materialised out of the dark bushes and startled Penelope so much that she screamed.

"Really sir, how rude of you to startle us like that. What nonsense are you talking? I was taught that in Heaven you would pretty well get what you want."

"No, it's not true. Tea is a stimulus and something not necessary."

"Go away you impertinent man!" What he said rattled Veronica because in her life tea was the high point of the day. It was only second to hearing a very good scandal, and the best times occurred when she was drinking a good cup of tea and hearing or sharing a good scandal. It had been her only pleasure.

Veronica and Penelope reached the centre of the garden.

"What do we do next?" asked the uncertain Penelope.

"We kneel down and wait." Veronica had sense enough to assume a repentant posture. She was anxious to get the formalities over with so she could quickly take her place in Heaven. Nothing happened for a long time. Penelope started to complain:

"I'm getting tired waiting here. Are you sure anyone will come?" The question vexed Veronica. She didn't have an answer. She could always pretend she knew what she was doing on Earth, but here one couldn't pretend for long.

"I was thinking, Veronica, perhaps it's that we aren't truly sorry for anything we did. The more I think about our gossiping the more I'm sorry we did it." Veronica stood up and faced her friend in astonishment. Penelope had never taken the lead before in their conversation. Somehow, she had changed. At first, Veronica was going to argue the point but then she became aware where she was. To her amazement, her friend prostrated herself on the ground and began to a weep passionately for forgiveness. Veronica was desperate to stop her friend from behaving so emotionally. Something though froze her into position and all she could do was watch.

As she watched a black grey, cloud came between her and Penelope. The chill penetrated through her entire body and with it a fear as to what was to come. A rasping voice whispered:

"Don't give in. Be your own person."

The advice was hardly necessary. She always tried to do what she thought best for herself. Gradually the grey cloud evaporated allowing her body to warm up. She saw herself walking down a corridor in her secondary school. She looked at herself with a hateful disdain. She was skinny with an asymmetric angular face. Blemishes covered her skin and her hair was thin and straggly. No wonder the boys rejected her. She saw two boys approaching her, one was small and stupid, and his companion was big and fat. Both were the targets for derision. Like so many people the others reject, he and his friend had to find someone else to hurt. The smaller boy confronted her in the crowded corridor.

"God, Veronica, that's an ugly dress. But it does go well with the rest of you."

Veronica pursed her lips as if to spit on the smaller boy.

"What would a stupid creature like you know about taste?" She turned and walked away from the two boys who attempted to laugh at her but knew that she had the better of them. Unfortunately, rude boys often accosted her and therefore she had an arsenal of acid replies for her attackers. The affect of this was at times devastating to those who were foolish enough to confront her.

In this case, Veronica now had to watch the smaller boy go home that morning. The phrase, 'stupid creature' resonated through his brain. No one was home since both parents worked. He opened the door and went straight to his parents' bedroom where he found his mother's sleeping pills. He swallowed the twenty pills that were in the bottle and died soon after. The whole school had been in shock at the boy's suicide. Veronica felt nothing. She had smiled maliciously to herself on hearing about the boy's death.

Veronica now knew that she was partly responsible for the boy's death. The implication of what she saw was quite clear, but she pretended that there was nothing to answer for. Was she now sorry for her part in his death and was she ready to forgive him for what he did to her and the many others like him?

Veronica's silent response was to justify her position. Who made her the ugliest and most despised girl in her school? If she were pretty and graceful like Amada Dalton, the most popular girl in the school, she would have never needed to defend herself from the school's scum.

Veronica concentrated on her studies. If she couldn't succeed socially, she would succeed academically. She won a teacher's scholarship to the local college. There no one mocked her or made fun of her. A few even respected her for her intellectual abilities.

One young man, Melvin, actually took a liking to her. He was a shy and quiet man who had a love of literature. Veronica found herself liking the young man despite her general hatred of men. She, though, hadn't developed the social skills to respond to his awkward overtures. Melvin managed the courage to ask her out for a cup of coffee. The evening went relatively pleasantly though there were many moments of silence when neither one knew what to say. While Veronica was sitting with Melvin, Mary Evans, who occupied a room next to her, walked by. Mary was attending the university mostly to have a good time and, with a bit of luck, to pass a few exams. She had plenty of money and good looks to achieve her goal. She looked on Veronica as stayed and stuffy. As Veronica was walking to her room that evening, she encountered Mary and three of her friends.

"I thought you hated guys, Veronica. What's this between you and Melvin? Do I see a romance in the making?" Veronica, who really liked Melvin, feared that others might see this.

"He's just a friend. We were discussing some plays by Oscar Wilde "

Mary was in a playful mood, so she pushed her point home.

"I think he's rather cute. I suppose you wouldn't mind me asking him out."

What she said threatened Veronica. She knew that she was no competition for Mary Evans. She could easily attract any boy she wanted to.

"Do what you like. It's a free country." She later bitterly regretted what she had said. She thought that she would never ask Melvin out or even get a response from him. But Mary was a pro at manipulating the opposite sex. She told her friends of her plan to seduce poor Melvin and then report back her success to

Veronica. To Mary it was all a bit of fun and a challenge. Mary was not worried about losing her virginity. She had lost it when she was twelve!

Mary began studying Melvin's daily routine always watched in the distance by her three friends. She rightly judged that Melvin had no idea who she was since he spent most of the time in the library, a place Mary usually tried to avoid. It was in the library then that she had to stalk her prey. She decided to dress deliciously drab even to the extent of borrowing a pair of thick glasses from a friend. She brought along her textbooks and for several weeks sat across the table from Melvin's usual place. She ignored him the first night and on the second night, she gave him a practised sweet smile.

It was late autumn and the nights were drawing in. She decided to make her first move on the third night. She had told her friends that she would seduce Melvin in less than two weeks time. Veronica had come to the library that very night and when she saw Melvin and Mary studying together, she left immediately. Mary knew that Melvin left at precisely nine o'clock. She got up just two minutes before nine and paused at the library door knowing he would soon come.

As he came out, she spoke to him:

"Hello, I wonder if you could do me a favour." Melvin was startled that a young lady would even speak to him.

"Yes, what would you like?"

"Well as you can see it's getting dark and I am really nervous about walking across campus at night. I heard rumours that there is a man who, well you know." She pretended that she was too shy to say anything. She wished her friends could see her great performance.

"I was wondering if you could walk me to my dorm tonight." She held her head down coyly glancing over her thick glasses.

Poor Melvin was completely taken in. He gratefully walked Mary to her dorm. In response, Mary gave Melvin a little kiss. By the third walk home, Mary had Melvin's hormones in full drive. She achieved her objective in twelve days. Her efforts and success had been monitored by Veronica who not only saw Mary take Melvin by the hand into her room, but she was able to take photographs of what went on through an open window.

Once he was conquered, she immediately dumped the confused Melvin. Veronica never spoke to Melvin again for allowing Mary to seduce him. Rather than being sympathetic, she hated him for his weakness. She waited for the right time to have her revenge on Mary. It came one year later when Mary was engaged to a promising senior at the university. She was in the throws of her wedding plans when her fiancée confronted her with a photograph of her leading Melvin to her room. He, by no means a virgin, was determined to marry an unspoilt woman. He cancelled the wedding and Mary left school in a state of shock.

Veronica again was unrepentant. What did she do wrong? She merely sent a photograph of an event, which really happened. She did not lie or distort the truth. She saw herself as saving a young man from a conniving woman.

She studied to be a teacher, but she found that she could not do so. She didn't like the children who she found constantly tried to make fun of her. She ended her career as a school librarian where she carefully watched over the books and dismissed anyone who attempted to make the least amount of noise.

David Triton, a young good-looking English teacher, often came to the library. He was always polite and courteous to Veronica. He came on a Wednesday evening and often chatted with her about the books he read. He appreciated Veronica's understanding of literature. She treasured the short moments they had together. This lasted for six months until he met Betty Andrews who was an attractive young married teacher who just had joined the school. Veronica, of course hated the girl since as soon as she came the sessions that Veronica had treasured with the young man stopped.

Betty came with him to the library, according to David, so that they could more effectively team-teach their subject. She searched discreetly for any signs of inappropriate behaviour. One evening she was certain she saw his hand over hers across the library table. She was a married woman allowing a single man to hold her hand. This was the damning evidence she was looking for. She puzzled for a long time as to how to use this information to stop the two's unseemly behaviour.

Her solution was simply to have a quiet word with the headmistress.

The headmistress came in once or twice a week. She saw her come in the following Thursday and then decided to approach her.

"Miss Taggart could you be so good as to come into my office. I would like to talk to you in private." Miss Taggart was traditional headmistress who liked to keep a tight control over her school. She was fair but she tolerated no nonsense.

"Well Miss Stillwater how can I help you?"

"I'm concerned about David Triton and Betty Andrews. You may or may not know that they have been meeting in the library and the other day he held her hand."

"Miss Stillwater this is the twentieth century. Secondly, a man may touch another woman's hand and not necessarily be making a play for her. If they gave you the wrong impression, they may have given others the wrong impression. I would ask your discretion in this matter and would ask you not to repeat what you have seen to anyone."

"Certainly, Miss Taggart, I won't say a word to anyone." Veronica knew that this would be difficult. She had to tell someone.

It didn't take long for her to break her promise, at least in principle. Mrs Jackson was another member of the English department. She happened to come in on a Wednesday when Triton and Betty were sitting across from each other at their usual table. They were leaning over and discussing a point quietly and once again Triton held her hand. This was not a sign of endearment it was only his way of expressing himself. He was a very tactile person. Both Mrs Jackson and Veronica were watching when they made the fatal touch.

"Did you see that? I was just talking to Miss Taggart the other say about this very same thing. It really should be stopped."

"I think you mean he should be stopped." Mrs Jackson had no love for Triton. She was envious of his popularity with the students.

Three weeks later the school dismissed Triton from his job for reasons not made public. Betty quit her job and because of the so-called scandal, her marriage broke up.

This time a voice thundered an accusation:

"You were responsible for the suffering of these people. What do you have to say for yourself?"

"I did not intend to hurt Triton. I'm terribly sorry he had to suffer. It was his fault. As for ruining Betty's marriage, Veronica felt no guilt. Betty had been the married woman who was not satisfied with just the company of her husband. She had to have David too.

The mist once again engulfed her and the cold bit painfully' yet she stood her ground and did not repent. The mist cleared and she found herself comfortably warm watching herself and Penelope having tea in Haversay.

"Penelope, you'll never guess who I saw entering Maggie O'Hare's cottage last night." They could see the front door of Maggie's cottage from their house.

"Why should I care who goes into her cottage. I'm sure no one cares who comes to ours."

Penelope always claimed a disinterest in the latest gossip; but it was all playacting. "Well if you don't want to know then I'll not say anything." There was a slight pause in the conversation both women waiting to see who would give in first.

This time Veronica succumbed:

"Would you believe I saw Ronald Wright coming out of her cottage ten o'clock at night!"

"Well I never. And he's a married man with two lovely daughters."

"Yes, it's shocking what people get up to."

"Poor Mrs Wright, she probably thinks nothing is wrong with her marriage. You would have thought that Maggie had done enough damage already. Tom Wallace is in trouble with his wife over her." Of course, the reason that he did get in trouble was that Veronica let it be known that Tom was there late one evening. Neither man's business was anything below the board. Tom came to help Maggie with some repairs because he felt sorry for her and Ronald fixed her television. Veronica's gossip condemned both men and Maggie. Now she was made to watch Ronald and Tom while they were in Maggie's cottage. Again, Veronica was unrepentant.

"All I did was mention to a few ladies what I saw. It wasn't my fault they thought the wrong thing." She spoke to an unseen presence that she knew was there. There was no response.

The mist cleared away and she found herself once again in the garden. Penelope had vanished. Veronica knew that she had seen all she would be shown. She also knew that she must repent for the pain and suffering she had caused to others because of her gossiping. Yet she knew she still had a chance to ask forgiveness. She wasn't sure though that she wanted to. She took a different path out of the garden then she had come down. She didn't want to return to the table she had left from especially with a Bishop and a priest waiting there. She emerged from the garden feeling young and sensual and as if bidden by her now lustful feelings a young man appeared before her. Veronica felt strongly attracted to the handsome young man.

"Veronica, I think I know where you want to go. After all there is no sex in Heaven and with a young attractive body like yours it would be a waste." Veronica at first was ready to challenge the young man for his sarcastic remark but he produced a handheld mirror embroidered in gold and in it she saw a beautiful woman with a remarkably beautiful body. She took the young man's hand and he led her away. She was waiting for this moment for all eternity.

At the table, Fr. Michael and the Bishop were waiting with the arms dealer and the advertising executive. The weather had turned for the worst. The cold grey mist was halfway across the lake. Fr. Murphy looked at the Bishop who still appeared as indecisive as ever. He finally got up and with a determined stride headed towards the garden.

David Foulgate then spoke: "Now, I wonder what that priest did to take him so long to go to the garden. He couldn't have been as bad as us."

The Bishop spoke on behalf of Fr. Michael: "Fr. Michael has waited here for the same reason I have. Both of us are teachers and according to the scriptures teachers will be judged more harshly than others because we should have known what was right and wrong since this is the very thing we had taught other people."

Fr. Murphy prayed for the strength to make it to the Garden. He was well aware that he fell short of the tasks, which God had given him. He felt his legs grow weaker and weaker. Fear once again paralysed him as it had just before his breakdown.

Chapter 15

TRUST ME!

Fr. Murphy was always haunted by the fear of failure. His father was a strict disciplinarian who gave his children little encouragement. He was a man who hated boys who behaved like sissies. The boys learnt never to complain to him about any problem. He would not even allow their mother to give them comfort. In his stupidity he believed that a man never whimpered or complained and should never, under any circumstances cry.

One summer's evening a fierce thunderstorm struck Michael Murphy's village in southern Ireland. The winds hit gale force in minutes catching both man and beast by surprise. Michael had left his window open and ran upstairs to his room to close it with his older brother close behind. Michael opened the door of his room and went straight to the window. As it snapped shut, he sighed with relief for the rain quickly came down in torrents. His relief was short lived for when he turned back from the window, he saw an enormous black bird. It screamed at him with its sharp beak snapping and its black eyes flashing.

His older brother, out of fear, ran from the room closing the door behind him. The black bird frightened him so much that he refused to open the door despite his brother's screams of terror. The bird and the boy were trapped together in the small room. Agitated by the boy's screams the black bird attacked him with talon and claws digging into his flesh. The older brother hearing his brother's screams and the frantic beating of the bird's wings finally shouted for help. His father rushed up stairs and pulled the older brother away from the door. He grabbed the black bird and quickly snapped its neck.

The bird lay dead on the floor its wild eyes still wide open. Rather than comfort his child the father remarked sternly:

"How could you have been afraid of that small lump of a bird?" He then left the room leaving the boy with the dead monster.

Years later he still had nightmares of that day. In his nightmares a large black bird would have him trapped in a cave, a room or even a cage. He was always paralysed with fear and while the black bird would attack him without mercy trying to gouge out his eyes. He would awake with screams of terror. His father would send his mother up to shut him up. She was more than fed up with his nightmares after several years of them. The family refused to have him see a psychiatrist since they and their friends knew that only crazy people needed them.

Michael learned to live with his nightmares and somehow, though still terrified while having them, learnt to wake up without screaming. A kind and holy priest, Fr. Benjamin, convinced him that praying for deliverance of the nightmares would work. More importantly, he convinced him of the truth of St. Paul's statement from Roman Chapter 8, :'Now in all things we are more than conquers through him who loved us. For I am convinced that neither death nor life, neither angels or demons, neither the present the future or any powers, neither height or depth, nor anything else in creation, will be able to separate us from the love of God that is in Christ Jesus our Lord.' It was this priest who convinced him that God would never let him down and inspired him to become a priest.

Michael wanted to be just like this priest. He went to the seminary where Fr. Benjamin taught and was very happy for the first two years. His joy was increased by his parent's pleasure with his academic success and the status that he gave the family by becoming a priest. They themselves were Catholics in name only. Sadly, they had no deep faith.

One cold grey winter's day Michael received word that Fr. Benjamin had suffered a serious heart attack and was in danger of dying. With great faith Michael prayed and his feelings were so strong that he announced with confidence that Fr. Benjamin would be all right. Those who heard him say this became very concerned since they knew how much he loved and needed Fr. Benjamin.

Fr. Michael saw himself praying for Fr. Benjamin's life and cried as he watched.

"Oh, God why didn't you answer my prayers. I needed him. If only you could have let him live a little longer, I might have had the strength to continue on my own?"

No answer came. He had to watch himself enter the black despair he had felt after Fr. Benjamin's death. He watched as the kindly rector, Fr. Adrian, came to his room to console him. He refused to be console.

"Why did God take the only true friend I ever had? If you can't tell me then please leave my room." Fr. Adrian knew it was of no use to speak to the boy in his state, so he left the room to go to the chapel.

Fr. Michael was shown how Fr. Adrian had fasted and prayed for him night and day for several weeks and in that he had his answer. There was someone to take Fr. Benjamin's place as a friend. A man who was filled with love and faith, but Michael didn't want him. He refused this great grace offered to him and instead suffered a deep depression. He now saw that God's love was there for him if only he would have accepted it.

The past faded into mist and he once again found himself on the Garden path. He started again with renewed strength but with a new urgency for the Garden was dying before his eyes. The trees' leaves were falling, and some trees were bowing and falling rotten to the ground. It was as if death had taken control of all living things. A new and threatening darkness engulfed Fr. Michael as he struggled to make it to the centre of Gethsemane. The ground shook slightly, and he began to run. Five enormous black birds as big as men suddenly blocked the path. One stood directly across the path its wings spread ready to attack. The old fear began to creep back into Fr. Michael's soul. The bird blocking his way began to speak:

"Look around you puny man. You can't escape us, and either can you escape the fate of your soul. Death itself is in charge here now. Your God has deserted you in his own garden and left us here to devour you."

The black birds came forward and as they did so Michael tried to turn and run but he found that fear had paralysed him and to his horror the path beneath him was turning into mud. In a short agonising moment, he had sunk to his knees and was surrounded by the ugly birds that were now jumping up and down ready to taste his blood.

"His eyes are mine," shouted the leader.

In anguish he screamed, "God help me," and in an instant he found himself at the centre of the garden safe and at peace. An angel stood in the middle of the garden whose love Michael could feel.

"Michael the birds which you saw were only in your mind. They never existed. If you had learnt to trust in your loving God you would never have had to suffer them. He loves you Michael and he wants you to trust him."

Michael threw himself on the ground and wept for forgiveness and also in joy for those were the words that made him more than anything else want to follow Jesus.

"Now look on the rest of your life in the light of His love. He was always there Michael, but often you ignored Him and His love."

His next crisis came the summer before he was to graduate from the seminary. The summer term before he left on holiday he went to the local town to the cinema with a friend, Tom Edwards, who also was graduating that year. His friend was an inspiration to him. He was handsome and talented in every way. He was popular with the staff as well as the other students. Michael felt honoured that he would want to go out with him, a poor country bumpkin.

It was a beautiful spring day filled with the smells of freshly cut grass and gardens in bloom.

Michael and Tom stopped at a nearby coffee shop to have some coffee before the cinema. There, to Michael's surprise, Tom met two girls that he knew and introduced them to Michael. One of the girls, Betty, was eighteen and was going to a college not far from the seminary. She had a flat of her own with her flatmate, Alice, who was up in London for a wedding. Betty invited all of them to her flat. She said she had a more interesting video to watch there than was playing at the cinema. Tom agreed immediately and looked to Michael for his approval. Michael was extremely nervous about the prospect but, like all young people, didn't really want to look like he wasn't with it. He was hoping though to get a chance to talk to Tom alone. He wanted to ask him if the girls really knew that he was studying to be a priest. If they didn't, then something could happen that they might regret.

Once in the flat Betty offered everyone drinks. Michael was become more and more agitated. He never was this close to two girls his age before and certainly never in a girl's flat drinking alcohol. He was in a pure panic when the video began with several scenes of explicit sex. Betty began to cuddle up to Tom and Michael was surprised that Tom encouraged her.

Betty then had a quiet word with her friend Sarah. Sarah then suddenly announced that she had to go home, as it was nearly ten o'clock. She smiled sweetly at Michael:

"Michael, could you please walk me home. It's very dark out there and I would be nervous walking by myself. Before Michael could reply Tom spoke.

"I'll see you back at our place Michael. I might be getting back late so if you could see your way through to signing me in. I'd appreciate it."

"Sure," is all he could say. He wanted to scream a protest, but he felt he was already involved in the night's activities and had fully compromised his principles.

It was the perfect night to walk an attractive girl home and Michael was all too aware of it. The fragrance of the spring blossom and the full moon gave the night an added enchantment. Sarah, who worked in the college town as a secretary, lived in a flat near its centre. The village pond was on the way there. It had a very convoluted shore that in many places was covered by willow trees. This made it a favourite trysting place for local lovers. Even Michael was aware of its reputation.

It was Sarah who first broke the silence as they walked. "What it's like studying in a seminary. Do you have the same courses as they do in the college?" Michael was aroused from his thoughts of guilt by her question.

"How did you know I went to the seminary?" He was worried that he appeared very naive and inexperienced.

"I know Tom goes to the seminary and that you are living with him so it doesn't take a genius to work out that you must go there too."

"But how did you know Tom goes there?"

"He told Betty years ago. It's strange that she keeps on seeing him."

"Seeing him?" Michael couldn't believe that one of the seminary's star students had a relationship with a girl.

"And their relationship isn't platonic." Michael was in shocked silence as he took in the information. One thing he despised more than anything else was hypocrisy but he, like many young people, often confused hypocrisy with a weakness. Sarah continued:

"Betty and Tom were close before he went into the seminary. She likes him very much and refuses to get another boyfriend which I think is very silly."

They walked a bit making small conversation that Michael was never good at.

"Let's go and sit near the pond awhile. It's really a beautiful night and you can tell me what's like living in the seminary," suggested Sarah. Michael now intoxicated by the warm spring night and the girl beside him found he was saying yes. Simultaneously he prayed not to be led into temptation but as he walked to Sarah's favourite spot, he knew his prayers were not from the heart.

They lay down in a place completely hidden behind the trees with only the ducks in the quiet waters of the pond to act as sentinels. He allowed Sarah to sit very close to him and his body temperature was rising to maximum.

"I was watching you when you were looking at the video. I could tell that you were very embarrassed. I don't think you ever had sex with a girl before."

"Of course not," was Michael's instant reply. He was sorry in one way that he had answered so quickly. Now Sarah knew that he was a naive seminarian with no experience.

Sarah gently pushed her point forward:

"How could you counsel other couples on sex if you have no experience yourself."

"You don't have to do it to understand the psychology of it." Sarah didn't reply but she looked into Michael's eyes telling him he could soon have the experience he wanted. He often wondered what it would be like and he often thought how uncomfortable he would be trying to perform with no experience. He tried to push those thoughts out of his mind knowing that they were sinful. But it was too late his urgings were in full control.

One voice was telling him that he would feel terrible after such an act. The other voice mocked him and pointed to the fact that at this very moment Tom was no doubt engaged in the very same act.

After that night with Sarah, Michael was no longer an inexperienced boy.

Michael couldn't go to communion for weeks after he had compromised himself. He was upset with his confessor for making light of the situation by telling him that it was just natural curiosity, which drove him to commit this sin. The confessor tried to tell him that it was the girl he should be praying for. He didn't have sex alone. Michael was more concerned with the stain on his soul and the fact that he had shown a weakness then with the affect of this act on Sarah. Michael once again went into depression and once again the symbol of his defeat in life, the blackbird, dominated his dreams.

Michael understood that it wasn't God who was tormenting him for what he thought of as his greatest sin. He was tormenting himself. Also, he had completely missed the point of what sex was all about, an expression of intimate love and the possibility of a new life.

Fr. Michael then saw something that shocked him more than any life's experience. He was allowed to see Sarah eight month's after the night he had sex with her. She was obviously pregnant!

"Was that my fault?"

A kindly voice responded:

"Yes, Michael it was. And the child she bore is your son. He's still alive and well today. All this time you were more concerned about how your sins affected you, not others. She suffered greatly to carry your child. And the child has had to live without a father for a long time. But now Sarah is happily married to a man who loves her and your son."

"I don't think I ever could have resisted her on that night."

"Yes, you are right. You yourself could never resist a temptation. But if you had allowed our loving God to assist you, you would have prevailed. He loves you Michael and he always has even through the last and the worst nightmare of your life, your break down."

It was Michael's first parish. He was so anxious to be a good priest showing his father and mother how good he was. But he wanted to help those in his parish, both young and old to find God and to be a part of all their lives from baptism to the grave. He would be the loving and kind priest who would help them and who they would look up to in their time of need. He would be just like Fr. Benjamin.

Though Fr. Adrian tried to warn Fr. Michael of the politics of parish life he took little heed. The parish where he was going was really two parishes. One group of people, many who were older, liked the quiet Mass. They believed that their faith was a private affair between them and God, and that the idea of community was something invented by the Protestants. The other faction liked a lively Mass often with drums and tambourines, believed in community and some belonged to a small charismatic prayer group who some members of both groups called the happy clappers. Fr. Michael was undeterred by the knowledge of this faction and gave little notice to the fact that the previous priest asked, or to be precise, begged to be moved away from this Church. He was tired of all the bickering and quarrels between so called Christians.

The different groups watched Fr. Michael carefully to see which camp he was in. Fr. Michael was careful not to take any sides. In fact, when he realised how polarised the groups were, he planned his sermons entirely differently for both masses being very careful not to offend either group. The results were his sermons were deadly boring and his loving parishioners were not too timid to let him know. Fr. Michael was quickly realising that he could not please everyone.

It was after his last mass on Sunday that Jim Durman came by to see him. Jim was a pious man who was graced with more than an average amount of wisdom. He was concerned about Fr. Michael particularly as the last priest found the parish so difficult, he asked to leave.

"Good morning, Fr. Michael, I was wondering if I could have a chat with you."

"Hello, Jim, I hope you don't have a complaint about my sermons. That's all I seem to get these days."

"So you find us a bit difficult, do you?" Jim was hoping that Fr. Michael would share his problems with him He had an excellent knowledge of the scriptures and had written a book called, 'The Gospel Message - The Best Book on Practical Psychology'.

"I suppose not really. I would have to say I don't feel I've found my feet yet. But in time I'm sure I'll be all right."

"If there is any way I can help please let me know. I would like to support you in any way that I can. You have a damn difficult job here. In fact, I might even call it impossible."

Fr. Michael was really depressed. He didn't want to let anyone know how down he was. After all, wasn't he God's priest sent to this parish to help and serve the people? What would they think if they knew that their pastor and spiritual leader was depressed and bewildered?

"I'm going to give you some advice whether or not you want it. Father, don't try to please everyone. All you have to do is do what you think God wants you to do and say. It's very difficult to listen to God but there is no other way that you can be a good pastor to your people. My favourite passage from the bible on this topic comes from Matthew chapter 11.

Come to me all you who are weary and burdened, and I will give you rest. Take my yoke upon you and learn from me, for I am gentle and humble in heart and you will find rest for your soul, for my yoke is easy and my burden is light.

"On a lighter note Jane and I would like to invite you to dinner. I will not have any hidden agenda of more advice or counselling. But I would like to say that my wife and I are here for you if you need us."

"Thanks very much Jim," said Fr. Michael sincerely. He really wished he could have bared his soul to Jim, but he was just a layman. But deep in his heart he knew that Jim was a man who had first-hand experience of God the way that he, as a priest, should have. Yet his pride would not let him admit this fact to Jim.

The kindly voice then questioned Fr. Michael:

"Why didn't you take your friends advice to listen to the Master? Why didn't you trust the One who loved you more than anyone else in the world?"

"My faith was weak. I needed assurances. I needed someone or something I could hear with my human ears, touch with my human hands and see with my human eyes."

"Turn to Him now, Michael. I am going but if you want, He will come and you will know what you could have had on earth."

Chapter 16

The Bishop's Turn

Remaining at the table was Phil Earl, the advertising agent, Bishop John Devon and Charles, manager of the El Faro restaurant. The table was sheltered under a large tree from the rain that was now starting to fall. The thick black clouds swirled threatening those beneath them. A funnel appeared on the opposite shore of the lake. As it moved into the water, a spout began to form. Those remaining knew that they must make a decision and soon.

Phil Earl was the first to speak. "I was hoping that someone would come along and offer me a position. It looks like I'll have to make the first move." Two men instantly appeared.

"Well gentlemen, it looks as if you're the last ones on this island before it's demolished. I take it that you are coming with us. It was you, I believe Phil, who called us. Are you ready to join us then?"

Phil responded with one eye nervously on the ever-growing waterspout:

"I was hoping you could offer me some type of position in the line of work I'm now doing, advertising. Am I correct in assuming that you do this type of thing quite often?"

One man looked at the other and smiled: "I told you David that this man has promise."

The other man smiled at David. Their manner was of men discussing a simple business deal, not the eternal fate of a soul.

"Well Lenny, after all you said this man had been working for us all his professional life. He's the one who convinced so many of our present guests that they needed the latest gadgets and material comforts. His encouragements bankrupted many of our guests. More importantly, he encouraged others to indulge in their own desires and comforts. He would be an excellent asset on our next island."

Their accusations surprised Phil: he was just a good advertiser, the best in the business.

"I don't think it was my fault that my targets overspent. How they spent their money is surely their responsibility."

The Bishop then responded:

"Don't you feel that one is responsible for what one says?"

"Also, Bishop, one is responsible for what one doesn't do or say. Wouldn't you agree?" said Lenny knowing too well the Bishops shortcomings while on Earth.

The Bishop responded with a sigh of resignation:

"That's why I cannot go to my Master. I should have been the servant to the poor and downtrodden. I misused by power and I must pay."

Two of His helpers appeared as a brilliant light burst around them:

"Why not ask his forgiveness, you still have time. He is the Good Shepherd always ready to forgive those who sincerely ask him."

Dave laughed:

"They don't really know that you can be forgiven. We know how you threw the trust of the Master back in his face and pretended to do the right thing. I'm sure we will see you later Bishop. There are a few Bishops where we are, and we always have openings for more. We'd better be on are way Phil. I'll introduce you to your supervisor and you can get to work shortly."

"Do you have any convincing slogans ready? He likes a man who can think for himself."

"Firstly, I would never refer to Hell itself. It just has a bad reputation. I would emphasize, like any good salesman, the competitions bad points. First, it is a well-known fact that in heaven you are not your own man. In heaven you have to do the unselfish thing no matter how hard it hurts."

"That's good Phil," encouraged David.

"What other advantages are there?" asked Lenny.

"Well one of the big draws on Earth is sexual pleasure. We know that because we constantly use it in advertising. As an example, when cars are advertised, we use the idea, as stupid as it is, that owning our car can make you more attractive. So, what I'll sell is perfect sex for as long as one wants it. For we all know that there is no sex in heaven."

"Yes, but what people don't realise is that constant pleasure of any sort will end up extremely boring," remarked the Bishop.

"Is this from experience Bishop?" The three men laughed derisively.

"Bishop you really must make a move soon. You're losing time." The helpers were becoming very anxious.

"No, Bishop, please stay. I have one sales pitch especially for you." The Bishop looked suspiciously at Phil.

"The one thing that's going to stop many people like you is that they're going to have to face all the people who are in heaven whose lives they made a misery. Can you imagine Hitler in heaven? What is he going to say to the millions of people who he had killed, whose families he destroyed?" The Bishop listened to the young man amazed at his hostility towards him.

"Do you remember me?" The Bishop looked at the young man intently. "Ah, Fr. Phil Earl, you were the priest who I sent to a difficult parish in east London. Unfortunately, you had a nervous breakdown."

"Well done Bishop. I'm surprised that you remembered. As you say the parish was difficult."

Phil tried to hold back the rage that was in him:

"Yes, you might say the parish was difficult. Poverty was the main problem. My people had to live in high-rise flats whose connecting corridors the misguided covered in graffiti. The tenants had to face drug dealer and muggers to get to their flats. Once out they could get their dole payments and feel the guilt of being a parasite to the community. And then, there were the old people who told me of their constant fears of being mugged or raped by the young gangs that ran freely about the estate.

"The pain and frustration of these poor people was unbearable for me. I felt impotent, and when I came to you to ask for help both practically and spiritually you didn't have time for me. You were preparing yourself for a synod, which was the most important thing in your life. The great Pope called you and you had to go and drop all other insignificant problems like the poor and suffering in your diocese. It was then I realised that all I was doing was a waste of time one act of futility after another. And you, dear Bishop, helped make my decision to leave the priesthood. OK, gentlemen, I'm ready to leave. I'm sure the Bishop will be joining you soon. I am sure he has many acquaintances in Hell."

The Bishop looked at him sorrowfully:

"I'm truly sorry that I didn't give you the support you needed. I ask your forgiveness."

"Sorry Bishop, it's too late. You've lost my soul and countless others. Why should you get to heaven when you helped so many others go to hell by your selfish ambitions?" With that, Phil disappeared with his new associates.

"Bishop hurry, you don't have much time." The helpers looked on as the Bishop sat with his head down.

"He will forgive you. Just ask him. Turn to him."

"I was supposed to be the shepherd to His people. Do what he would have done for them. I have failed."

As he finished speaking a great blackness covered his eyes. A chilling cold paralysed him, and he feared that they had taken him to Hell. Quickly, the cold freezing darkness lightened to a white mist and gradually he could begin to see images through it. Bishop John Devon saw himself in his secondary school sitting in his physics class eagerly awaiting the teacher's questions. The subject was the formation of a star. Already John had a haughty attitude. He felt superior to both the teacher and his fellow students. He read ahead on the subject and he knew far beyond what the syllabus required. He would not hesitate, though, to interject a question that he knew the teacher couldn't answer to prove his superior knowledge.

Mr. Adams, the physics teacher, had just finished explaining the formation of a star. He then asked the class some questions to test their understanding. "Mary, can you tell me what two forces are acting on a new star?" Mary hesitated then answered. "Well one of the forces is gravity and the other, I think, is fusion. "

"Gravity is certainly one force Mary, but fusion is a process, not a force." He looked at the rest of the class ignoring John who he knew could name the other force. "Does anyone know the answer?"

John was waiting for Mr. Adams to ask him personally. Mr. Adams refused to give him the satisfaction this time. Reluctantly he answered the question in his usual condescending way.

"I don't know if there is another force but the process of nuclear fusion creates a lot of heat and hence cause the gases in the star to expand. This pushes the star outward while the force of gravity pulls the star together. Hence there is an equilibrium between the two processes."

"As usual you are correct, John. Now does anyone have further questions on the making of a star?" John was now able to show the teacher and fellow students that his knowledge extended beyond the GCSE level.

"After the hydrogen is used up in a star it expands and increases in size by several times. Why does it do that?"

Mr. Adams smiled knowingly. Ever since he had John as a student, he had to study his physics in greater depth. Fortunately, he was prepared for this question:

"I believe, John, the reason for the rapid expansion of a star which has used all its hydrogen is that the heat from its core causes the outer gas layer to expand causing the size of the star to increase by several times." John sat smugly in his seat happy in the knowledge that he had once again demonstrated his superior knowledge.

Bishop Devon was ashamed to see the blatant conceit he had as a young man. He realised now that he should have been thankful to God for all his gifts and only used them to help others, not to show off. He sat and watched his life unfold, his conceit and ambition growing day by day.

Then he watched himself sitting and listening to the final instruction for his confirmation.

The priest, Fr. Brennan was giving the class their instructions for the day itself:

"Now don't forget, my dear people, that when you kneel before the Bishop you must kiss his ring?"

Without thinking John responded:

"Why should we kiss his ring?"

Fr. Brennan was surprised that his prize student would question his instruction:

"The reason, John, that one kisses the ring of a bishop is to show respect for his office." John had no desire to kiss any one's ring especially as a sign of submission. It was then that he began to desire the lofty office of the bishop not to serve but to experience the power the prestige and the position. All would respect him.

Bishop Devon them heard a sad voice:

"John why did you not come to serve your Master? The office you had sought and won had grave responsibilities. Holding the crosier was the easiest part. Loving and serving those put in your care by the Master was the most difficult but yet it could have been the most rewarding."

The Bishop was ashamed by what he had seen.

"Oh God please forgive me," he cried falling down on his knees. His pain had not ended there. He was made to continue to watch his selfishness flourish. The next scene unfolded before him. It was his senior year in the seminary, and he was in the middle of taking his final exams. He knew if he did well, he would have a chance to study in Rome, the goal of many ambitious priests. Unexpectedly his mother called the night before one of his most difficult exams. His father had a heart attack and was in the intensive care unit in Guy's Hospital. It would have taken him over a half day to get to London from the seminary, which was in York. He carefully weighed what he should do.

"How bad is he Mother?"

"Bad, he's in intensive care. That to me is serious."

"I can't make it before tomorrow night. I have a very important exam to take." There was a long pause on the phone.

"He might be still alive I suppose. Do what you think is best," she said flatly and then hung up the phone.

"John, you could have postponed your exam. You knew your teachers would understand. Why didn't you?" the accusing voice said.

"I have no good reply to that. Once again, my ambition was my main motivation in life. I wish now that I went as soon as I could. At least I could have been with my Mother to comfort her when he died. I was a selfish fool."

The Bishop continued to view his ambitious life. He now saw himself in Rome learning from the world's greatest theologians. He was at the centre of power of the Roman Catholic Church and was increasingly aware of the role of politics there. He wanted to be a part of it. He continued to be the exemplar student making every effort to please the most influential people there. Every answer he presented in class and everything he wrote was always right in line with the teachings of the Church. He was determined to please his masters though that left little time to listen to his true Master.

One of his friends, Paul Glass, had a passion for the poor. He often quoted Matthew 25 when convincing his fellow students how important Jesus thought it was to help the poor and the downtrodden:

For I was hungry and you gave me something to eat, I was thirsty and you,
gave me something to drink. I was a stranger and you invited me in, I needed clothes
and you clothed me, in prison and you came to visit me."

During his spare time, Paul would visit the Roman slums with a Franciscan priest, Fr. Peter Tarrus, who devoted his life to the poor of the city.

"John, why don't you come down with me this Saturday and meet Fr. Peter and see some of the work he's doing with the poor."

"I have a term paper due on Monday. I don't know if I'll have the time." Paul knew of his friend's ambitions, so he then added.

"Monsignor Gianna feels that some practical experience helps make a good priest."

As predicted, Paul then got a more positive response from John. Monsignor Gianna was the man responsible for writing their final report with career recommendations.

"Let me see how I get on with my term paper. If I'm finished by Friday, I'll be able to go with you."

"Good, I'll let Fr. Peter know that you might be coming. He's always pleased when someone takes an interest in his work."

John did finally come to see how Fr. Peter was helping the poor. He was impressed with what he saw and with Fr. Peter's deep faith. He encouraged the people spiritually as well as gave them practical help. He helped some of the young to get into good Catholic schools and found rich patrons to fund their scholarships. He helped to found a medical clinic to provide for those who couldn't afford medical care. He found jobs for the unemployed and convinced the carpenters' union to fund a training facility for carpenter's apprentices. His work also exposed him to physical dangers. The Mafia had threatened him more then once for convincing their drug dealers to stop dealing and turn to God. One of those converts became a priest.

John spent an increasing number of Saturdays helping the poor with Paul and Fr. Peter. His academic achievements suffered but he personally did not care. He was happy with serving the poor, happier than he had ever been. He would have continued working for the poor if ambition had not raised its ugly head. Monsignor Gianna noticed that John's studies were not of the usual high standard. He called him aside to discuss this:

"John, I've been watching you with interest and what I've seen is a very good mind tempered with maturity. You have a good possibility of an excellent career. The Church needs intelligent young men like you. Lately, though, your high standard of work has fallen. I think I know why and I in no way doubt your motives. Fr. Peter's work for the poor is a service, which I commend highly and the experience you have had in helping him will be a positive aspect in your development, but don't let your studies go down because of it. We all unfortunately have to make painful decisions That's all I have to say."

"Does that mean I have to stop helping Fr. Peter?"

"I wouldn't say that. What I'm trying to say is that you will never come anywhere near holding a crosier if you don't do well academically. Good day John."

John knew the discussion had ended and that any further questions would only irritate the Monsignor. He was unaware at the time that God was calling him to a special service, one which would have brought him a great deal of fulfilment. Monsignor Gianna was clever in ending the conversation with hints that John could be a bishop. His lust for power and prestige won over his true calling. He only visited the slums twice after talking to the Monsignor.

The bishop watched the final stages of his life at the point were Fr. Phil came to him for help. He saw the young priest working in the London slums consoling a mother who had just lost her son in a gang fight. The fight was between two gangs who were vying for the same area where there was a lucrative drug trade. The real gangsters just watched and waited to see who would be the winners, these boys would work for them.

When Fr. Phil left the mother, it was dark. He knew that the muggers, gangs and various drug dealers would be out in the corridors of the dilapidated block of flats he called his parish. He usually was careful not to walk out at night. As he was walking down a particular dark tunnel, he heard the voices of several boys. He knew that if they saw him, he would be easy prey. He was not a small man. He weighed fourteen stones and was in reasonable shape, but he was unarmed and outnumbered. As he emerged from the dark tunnel, the boys saw him and immediately surrounded him. Fr. Phil was determined not show any weakness. He knew he would be beaten and perhaps killed but he would not give up. The leader of the gang Mickey stood before him. He was six foot four and weighed seventeen stones.

"Hey ain't you the priest. Have you saved anybody today?" Fr. Phil ignored the questions and tried to walk past the giant of a man.

"I asked you a question and I expect an answer." With that, he shoved Fr. Phil against a wall and pinned him there. He could feel the strength of the man and he knew he could do nothing.

"I went to see the mother of a boy who was killed by a gang of thugs," he spoke with contempt.

"I suppose you think I'm a thug. You're right. We all are. Unfortunately for you, we're kind of bored so you are going to supply us with some entertainment. I am asking you politely to take off your clothes."

Fr. Phil attempted to pray but couldn't. He was filled with despair, frustration and anger.

"Go to hell," he shouted. In response, the big man began pounding the priest until he fell nearly unconscious to the ground. He lifted Fr. Phil up. Blood was running from the several cuts on his face. His eyes began to swell. He could barely stand.

"I'm asking you again. Will you kindly take off all your clothes?"

Fr. Phil replied whispering through his busted lips, "No, I will not."

"You're spoiling my fun and that my friend is a non-starter." With that he started tearing the Priest's clothes off and once naked they made fun of him and abused him. The police found his battered body barely alive the next day. they took him to the hospital where he was put in intensive care.

"Fr. Phil was in hospital for two weeks and you never found the time to visit him. When he went to see you after all he had suffered, you never gave him any time. It was only after he wrote his resignation letter that you agreed to see him."

Bishop Devon fell on his face and wept bitterly:

"Oh God forgive me. I had no idea of the great pain I caused that young priest. I deserve Hell."

The spout was nearly on the shore of the Island. The helpers escorted the Bishop away. The ground shook and darkness engulfed the eastern side: time had run out. When the spout hit the land Charles, the El Faro manager, was sucked up into its dark mass. He couldn't decide where to go. The decision was made for him.   On the opposite side of the island, two groups were waiting to be taken to their eternal destinations, those who chose to live with God and those who preferred to live for themselves without God's love.

Chapter 17

ON EAGLE'S WINGS

Father Murphy had left the Garden of Gethsemane and a funnel of golden fire led him down a dark path. He felt the earth shaking under his feet and the wind blowing, sometimes with hurricane force. Yet, the funnel of light neither dimmed nor moved no matter how fierce the wind bore down on it. Branches and whole trees would sometimes fall down around him. Father Murphy wasn't frightened. He was now surer of his direction than ever before.

The sky continued to darken so much that Father Murphy wasn't sure if he could even see with the funnel of fire illuminating his way. He felt the wind coming from ahead freshen and he could see that the forest was thinning. He then heard the crashing of waves far ahead. He must be heading to a shore of the island, but he had no idea what would be there or what he had to do next.

The funnel of light continued forward, but he turned from it because he saw daylight to his left. Desperate to leave the oppressive darkness, he decided to ignore his guiding light. He emerged from the forest at the top of a cliff one hundred feet above a narrow-pebbled beach below. As he looked down, he could see the large waves crashing over the beach. To the right of the narrow beach there was a large flat reddish rock, which appeared to have people under it. He looked again and, ever so often, a person would come out from the safety of the rock and look around. After a short time, the person would go back. If he had shouted, he doubted those below would have heard him. He was too high up and the wind was too loud. He somehow knew that his destination was with those people, but the problem was how to get there. It would be unthinkable to try to climb down the slippery cliff with near gale force wind buffeting it constantly. There must be another way.

He looked to his left and he saw even higher cliffs. Perched on these cliffs were regal white eagles. These immense birds were pure white and looked to Father Murphy to be several times larger than a man. There was obviously no way to the beach going to the left. He looked to his right and to his utter amazement saw an immense ocean liner. The twenty-foot waves, which were swamping the small beach below, looked like ripples to this immense linear. On its side, someone had written in large red letters the word *Invincible*. The letters were so large Father Murphy could see it a half mile away! Perhaps, thought Father Murphy, that is where those people below should be going. Though somehow, he thought it odd that God would choose such a vehicle to carry his chosen people to their last destination.

He was right on that account. Those who had chosen self-reliance before God were using the vessel. One passenger was Veronica Stillwater who felt safe at least from the outside elements. She well knew though that the greatest danger lay with her fellow passengers. These had chosen to rely on themselves rather than God. And most of the people there, Veronica was sure, believed in survival of the fittest. Yes, she had no doubt as to where the real dangers lay.

She spent most of the morning making love to her new mate Pete, a young handsome man. He was tall and muscular and had jet-black hair. She herself had a beautiful body, as did most of the women there. There were the odd few who thought their previous earthly bodies were as beautiful as a body could get. In some ways, they were right for these women were the most sought after: the reason being that most of the other women looked the same, tall, thin and blond. In other words, most of the woman looked liked Veronica Stillwater and most of the men looked like Bill. The first shock of Hell was to see everyone the same and at the same time no one was special. Each couple looked like the other and it was almost a relief to see the few who had decided to keep their old looks.

Bill and Veronica tired of their passionate love making decided to indulge their appetites for food and went down to the dining room. There they dined on the best food placed perfectly on white tablecloth with silver cutlery.

"Why do all of us women look the same? I simply chose the body and features I wanted.   If I knew everyone was going to look like me, I would have chosen a different body."

"You chose the body they wanted you to. It's their little way of tormenting us. In the end, we will probably get sick and tired of our bodies and then want a different type. We may even be able to choose yet another type, for a price."

"You seem to know a lot more than me. How long have you been on this ship?"

"That's difficult to say. Time is immeasurable here. It just drags on endlessly."

"Why do you think they are treating us so well? I mean I was taught Hell was a place of punishment."

Bill looked at Veronica and laughed:

 "It is my dear girl. Oh, it really is. Do you know what I was when I was last on Earth? I was a psychiatrist. I understand how they are playing with us. They give us all these wonderful things so that when they take them away it's all the more painful."

"Oh, I see. When do they do that?"

"They do that when they want to or when we break the rules."

"What rules?"

"That is a good question. I really don't know the answer to that. If you look around you though you can see some of the people who have broken the rules. They are the ones serving us now. But there are others. This ship runs on steam and for that it has tremendously large boilers and they need fuel."

"You, mean they might use us to fuel the ship?"

"No, not in the way you're thinking. They make some of us shovel coal for as long as they want us to. At least that is the rumour I heard. The point is that we all know what we deserve. Eventually we will have to suffer. What's frightening though is for how long. Eternity is a long time."

Bill smiled as he watched Veronica squirm:

"As the old adage goes, 'Eat, drink and be merry for tomorrow you may die'. I have a feeling that in the end we are going to wish that we could die."

Another man who thought he had made the right decision boarding the *Invincible* soon found his mistake. Inspector Maxwell was on the upper deck in search of Dan Radcliff who he was convinced was there despite all denials from the officers of the liner.

"He must be here," he said in frustration to one bewildered officer. "Where else could he be? "

"We don't have everyone here," the officer replied officially, but I can assure that if he was killed by the terrible storm that hit England, he's either here now or over with the others. The fools hiding under a rock."

"If he's not here than there is no just God!" Maxwell was shouting now.

"I think you had better come with me," said the officer. "There are certain things, which we don't say here in public. I'm afraid you've broken the rules. You will have to pay the consequences."

Father Murphy looked away from the liner and glanced once again down to the people below. He wondered why the funnel of light led him to a dead end. If only he could talk to one of the people. He was sure that at least one of them would know how to get down from where he was. He decided to shout and if necessary, scream to get their attention.

He walked to the edge of the cliff, shouted and moved his arms. At first, no reply came from below. Then finally one person saw him and then several people waved at him. With this encouragement, he pointed to the cliff and shrugged his shoulders indicating he didn't know how to get down.

When the people thought they understood his message they pointed back to where he came from which puzzled Father Murphy. Didn't the light of God lead him to this spot.

After thinking about it, he decided it hadn't. It was he who turned away from the light. He remembered now. He went a

different direction then the light was going because it looked lighter than the other way and therefore more promising.
"It's been that way all my life," he said aloud. "God would ask me to do one thing and I would do another."

    He backtracked and once again found the trail and the funnel of light was patiently waiting for him. The trail continued in the direction of the *Invincible*. It then began to dip downwards at an increasing pitch. When it dipped to about sixty degrees Father Murphy had to lower his body and start sliding down on his bottom and back. The path then became less steep, but it then entered into a foul-smelling black tunnel. The stench was of decay and death. Father Murphy was glad that the flaming funnel was still lighting his way. Without its help, he was certain he would turn and run the other way. He passed by several skeletons whose grotesque features were revealed by the reflected light of the flaming funnel.

    Further along the tunnel, he was certain he heard noises and even voices. The light stopped at what looked like a dead end. He was shocked at the knowledge it had led him to a dead end. He stared at the solid wall in disbelief. Then his terrible nightmare once again took on flesh.

    "Well it looks as if this one is still alive," hissed one of the black birds.

    "This time we'll finish him."

    "You don't scare me. I know you're an illusion." Father Michael spoke with more bravo than belief.

    "Is that so my friend. Well then here's a little peck from an illusion." With that the black giant of a bird flew at Father Murphy lashing him with his razor-sharp peak. Blood squirted from the wound on his arm.

    Father Murphy once again fell into despair but only for a short moment.

    "My loving God allows his sons to be disciplined. If it pleases him, I will take anything you can give me."

    In unison, the birds screamed and disappeared. When he turned to the dead end, he saw light! He walked out onto the beach directly between where the *Invincible* was anchored and the large flat rock which sheltered the others. He stood looking one way then the other.

People were still queuing up to get on the ship. Four of them were from Haversay, Ruth Wright and her two daughters and Charles the manager of the *El Faro* restaurant. Mrs Wright, as usual, was getting very impatient. She grabbed her daughters and went to the head of the queue. A large, fat red-faced man stopped her. As he spoke it was apparent that half his teeth were missing.

"Excuse me your highness, what do you think you're doing." Mrs Wright was in the habit of bossing those she felt beneath her and of course that was almost everybody.

"We don't allow queue jumping here. That's breaking the rules. And we don't take kindly to those who break the rules." Poor Mrs Wright. She just couldn't help responding the way she did on earth. On earth, she could tell any number of people to do her bidding because there she had money. Here she had nothing. But the poor lady forgot that.

"Look, I'm not wasting my time on an imp like you. I want you to take me to the Captain or at best your supervisor."

"You want me to take you to my sergeant and tell him in so many words that you would like to come board with out waiting your turn."

"See girls, he isn't as stupid as he looks." The two girls were more aware than their mother that they were no longer on Earth and that things were different here. As usual they just followed her.

"Very well my ladyship. I will with pleasure take you to my sergeant. He was looking for people just like you." The people around them began to laugh knowingly. Mrs. Wright, for the first time, sensed that she had made a fatal mistake. They were led to a large wooden door which the red-faced man knocked on. From the inside there was a growl and then a roar.

"Who is it that dares to interrupt my nap?"

"It is I, the keeper of the queue and I have three queue jumpers with me." With the phrase, queue jumper, Ruth Wright knew that she and her daughters were in serious trouble. The door swung open and an immense man filled its frame. He was a hideous looking monster, bald with a pock-marked face.

"Well thank you my friend. I've been looking for just the right people for a particularly nasty job. The requirement for this job is for those who think they are better than the rest. For those who think some of us are scum to be used." Here he menacingly looked down on the three helpless women. His smile indicated that he was enjoying watching the mother and two daughters squirm.

"You have been sent here to learn humility and, unfortunately, this comes with the loss of dignity. You are going to be given a job that most ordinary women had to do about one a week. You will be doing it every day. Do you know what this job is? The one you may have for all eternity. Perhaps I exaggerate. You'll probably only have the job a thousand years."

Mrs Wright and her two daughters felt pure terror and revulsion at what he had said.

"Your job is to remove human waste of any kind when called upon day or night. You will have just enough help to get two hours break every twelve hours. Yes, you will be watched and the one who is in charge of the Lows, as you will be called, has the right to torture those who don't comply. Are there any questions?"

Ruth was about to protest but she knew better. Then she thought of bargaining, but what did she have to offer.

"Would you reconsider if we offered our ah..."

"You've got to be kidding. I have six wives and every one of them is far more appealing than you. Here you have nothing to offer anyone. Your money is gone and therefore you have no power. I suggest you get off to your new jobs now. I'm sure your supervisor will be happy to see you."

Ruth was now learning what the essence of Hell meant: a place without hope or love, a place where humans have no dignity and a place where existence means life with out a meaning.

One gaunt figure paced on the beach waving his arms and shouting at those on the ship.

"You all are doomed. The storm will swallow you all. I'm warning you. There is no where you can go." The gaunt man was Paul Thorne. The one who failed to warn those in England of the great storm, which killed so many thousands. The passengers laughed at him and cursed him.

"You should have warned your country men in England. We 're all dead here anyway! The guards immediately dragged him away. His prophetic words were not to be heard by many. For some knew that without God, there was no life.

Father Murphy headed towards the rock shelter. The winds had reached hurricane force. There were gusts up to one hundred miles an hour. He could hardly walk on the beach. When he reached the safety of the shelter, he saw Bishop Devon.

"What's happening. Why are we waiting helplessly under this rock? We will soon be destroyed." The roar of the sea made it impossible to talk without screaming. The huge funnel was almost upon them. It was hovering just above the cliff where Father Murphy had just stood. The chosen ones were not afraid. They knew God would save them. The funnel began tearing the cliff apart above there heads. Hugh boulders crashed down on the flat rock. Those on the *Invincible* stopped all their activities. They were waiting for the funnel to devour the chosen ones.

Charles had finally got on board and was watching with the rest what looked liked the end of those waiting under the rock:

"I'm glad I chose the winners. I always thought the universe was ruled by the survival of the fittest."

Another passenger joined in:

"All those myths about a loving God. Look at those poor suckers. They are going to get what they deserve, nothing." As they jeered and laughed, a small light appeared on the horizon over the sea. As the light grew, the funnel appeared to retreat away from those sheltered under the rock. The light kept on growing and then it was obvious to all it had the shape of a cross. The laughter on board the *Invincible* abruptly stopped.

Those sheltering under the rock now came out and raised their hands towards the cross.

"He's coming for us." shouted one. They all started praising God. As the cross came closer, it became apparent that it was not a light but a way to another place. A golden light surrounded the brilliant white outline of a cross. Through the cross, one could see bits of blue and green.

The Bishop shouted to the people. "Come let us go." He then started to lead the people into the devouring waves. He kept walking looking at the cross and ignoring the force of the dark waves which could easily crush any man.

This gave those watching from the *Invincible* the courage once again to jeer:

"Look they're being led into the water to drown. They're all going to be smashed by the waves. The pain they will suffer will be fun to watch."

As if in answer the wind started to blow fiercely against the ocean liner. Everyone rushed for the cover of the enclosed cabins. The passengers began to scream. "The funnel is headed our way!"

The frightened passengers screamed as they trampled each other to get into safety. The funnel, now an immense waterspout, hovered next to the ship. It pulled off the passengers outside like tiny pieces of paper in a gale. Then it hovered over the ship, growing larger and larger until the ship itself was a toy in comparison. The ship and all on board were lifted away to their well-deserved fate.

As a thirty-foot wave was about to cover the Bishop, a large white eagle lifted him up. Then another eagle picked up Father Murphy. The eagles lifted each member who had waited in faith under the rock towards the opening in the sky.

As father Murphy approached the opening cross, he saw blue skies and green gardens and people. One Man standing there seemed to be the source of all the light and next to Him, he saw Father Benjamin. Joy filled Father Murphy as his soul and new body journeyed to its purpose, to its Creator and to the One who loved him more than any man could love him. The One who died for him. The One who called him in love every day of his life.

He gives strength to the weary and increases the power of the weak.

Even youths grow tired and weary, but those who trust in the Lord

will renew their strength.
They will soar on wings like eagles. Isaiah 40

The end   Amen

www.ingramcontent.com/pod-product-compliance
Lightning Source LLC
Chambersburg PA
CBHW071508040426
42444CB00008B/1550